# *Haven't You Noticed My Charisma?*

The Columns & Photographs of
Charles P. Spataro

Library of Congress Card Number
2001119371

ISBN 0-615-11927-1

First Printing — 2001

Printed in the U.S.A. by
Morris Publishing
3212 East Highway 30
Kearney, NE 68847
1-800-650-7888

To Joella

they only listen,
you're the one singing along.

To purchase a copy of "Haven't You Noticed My Charisma," send your name, address, and a $12.00 check or money order to:

Charles P. Spataro
Hardin County Independent
P.O. Box 1117
Elizabethtown, KY 42702

Make payable to Charles P. Spataro.

---

Front and back cover photos & design by M. Joella Spataro

# Acknowledgements

I wish to thank Hardin County Independent Editor Gerald Lush for his words of encouragement ("Hey, it doesn't have to be art, it has to be on my desk Monday morning 8 a.m.!") And thanks to Shannon Boone for picking acorns out of the confetti. Great appreciation goes to Kenny Bird for technical expertise. Finally, a sincere thank you to the newspaper readers in Hardin County, Kentucky.

# Table of Contents

## Chapter 1 - Love is Like...



## Chapter 2 - A Season to Celebrate

## Chapter 3 - "Chuck"les

## Chapter 4 - For the Love of the Game



## Chapter 5 - Cove Columns

# Chapter One

# Love is Like...

# In a perfect world

These flowers are for you who called. You, calling to say you liked something I wrote, a phrase I raised to the low art of column writing. Was it something about sky casting (kite-flying) or migraine headaches (crosses we share) or some other obscure idea which now rests yellowing upon your refrigerator door?

You called and got my answering machine. I didn't answer. I almost never answer my phone. I hardly ever even open my mail. Instead I listen. I watch. I write. From time to time you (or someone) catches me at Kroger's or Winn Dixie to say there's a column of mine yellowing upon your refrigerator door. I smile thanks but little more. All the while thinking of the flower bouquet I wish I could hand you then and there.

*Photo by M. Joella Spataro*

But I never have any flowers on me in person. Never do. I can only write about them. Just as I have no words to say to you over the phone. My words are things I punch on a keyboard transcribed from a black Flair pen with hands that ache.

In a perfect world I wish we'd never meet anyway. Which is no great loss because as my wife says, "Chuck's usually not really there when he's in person, anyway." True I'm not. We both stand at aisle six in Winn Dixie as you say hello and kindly mention that my sky-casting column is scotch-taped on your refrigerator door. I nod a "thank you" but I'm really not there…

I'm back at my writing desk. I'm capturing how your nose began to run. How your coat collar needed mending. And that your voice sounded brave as spring daffodils. All the while you were saying (in that quiet, brave, daffodil voice) how I reminded you of your departed husband, dead these past four years, because he also flew kites, also loved baseball, or also hated computers…

In a perfect world we'd never meet. Or when we did I'd pluck a bouquet of yellow daffodils from aisle six, the flower mart, and hand them to you on the spot. Leaving, I'm afraid, you to pay for them.

And on my refrigerator door is the yellowing letter you sent, the one with a picture of your deceased husband flying a kite. In a perfect world I suppose I'd reply to your letter. But I won't. In a perfect world I'd respond to your message on my answering machine. Again, I never do.

But I thought of him this morning. And together this morning we watched the Big Blue Heron lift like an angel from Harmony Cove. Together we warmed our arthritic hands, crooked as claws, upon a hot mug of coffee before our writing. I asked him if the kite string ever stings his fleshy palms? And he smiles and sort of says yes, thanks for asking.

Together this morning he told me how much you liked the first flowers of spring. And how you and he both felt the best part of spring is saving bundles of bright, yellow daffodils from a nipping frost, bringing them inside in thick bouquets.

In a perfect world you'd have him still, clipping flowers together. And folks like me would return your phone calls. I should and I would, in a perfect world.

But take these newspaper flowers in place of perfection and understand when the phone doesn't ring, it's me. —*April, 2001*

# Dad's house is still alive

As my father ages, his body is growing as stiff as Frankenstein's.

This amazes me. My father had a lithe, athletic body. As a construction working man, he used to skip up a wobbling ladder carrying 100 pounds of tools and equipment on his back. As his small son, I'd accompany Anthony Spataro to Saturday morning work sites where I witnessed a nimble, tanned worker ripping apart roofs with his carpenter's claw hammer. My father reminded me of a bigger-than-life movie star, lightly stepping across a stage, dancing across rooftops.

But as a slight (is there such a thing?) stroke, a lazy son in Kentucky (I know he exists), and the steady march of time began taking their tolls, the rooftop actor's body began to stiffen. Today he can only talk about job sites where he once worked, about scaffolds he once climbed, and about the houses he once built.

My dad built hundreds of houses. Harnessing his own abundant energy he forged from lifeless scraps of wood, steel, and stone, spaces for the living. These places held as much of my father's sweat and blood as they held metal nails and wooden beams—at least as much, maybe more.

These days his body is swollen by arthritis and constrained with old age. He resembles more the Frankenstein monster than the fleet rooftop actor. He walks with one arm slightly lifted, as if reaching for something or someone. The stiff arm is a memento, the stroke's calling card, left behind as a reminder. It is hardly noticeable unless you had once seen that same arm balance gigantic weights of lumber, then, twist that lumber comically catching a ham sandwich lunch I'd toss up the ladder.

Some days I see faint glimpses of former dexterity. At a recent family reunion the old man fixed a wooden birdhouse so I could carry it back on the plane to Kentucky. His hands flashed across the wood, driving in wood screws and hammering nails. His face was once again the picture of concentration to task. I imagined the young actor Boris Karloff's face, buried deep beneath the wounds and scars of life's living makeup, and I saw the face faintly smiling.

*A-live, it is alive...*

After all those years, all those houses built, I wonder what part of life's drama (comedy or tragedy?) has my father lifting up a wooden birdhouse for his bald son to take home. And I wonder, "Was Frankenstein the name of the monster or its maker?" Author Mary Shelley knew the answer. And the young Karloff, whose monster was a mirror for millions of moviegoers, knew the answer.

And I suppose I am learning the answer as well. I am, after all, my father's son. My body has already begun its own stiffening process. Perhaps we were both in the construction business. Perhaps my rooftops have been tabletops piled high with pages of poorly written prose. What was true of the father is true for the son; each made a product intended for the living.

At 75, most of my father's living years exist in the century just expiring. At 46 it is quite possible the same may be said of me, but for now I sit on my back porch in Kentucky building a birdhouse, admiring its delicate construction. And I know one thing for certain. His house is still alive. *— October 1999*

# Grace

Sara close your eyes. Close them tightly and hold still as your sister brushes make-up and strokes eyeliner upon your gentle face before Central Hardin High's senior prom. Close your eyes kiddo and make a wish.

I'm here, the family uncle who takes photos. The old fart whose teary-eyed wife has lent the sparkling necklace hovering above that strapless, ice-cool, blue gown. I'm here wondering what you are thinking...

Perhaps you're wishing that by some miracle your dress will actually manage to stay upright the whole evening long...

Or you won't lose Aunt Joella's diamond earrings and necklace. Or won't fall in those death-defying-tall high heels, or, won't slip on the dance floor, and/or eat with the wrong fork at the fancy restaurant he's taking you to before the prom...

I'm snapping your photo now. You, in the ice-cool blue dress, you my niece whose soul springs from three Graces: Grace Kelly's cool blond beauty, Gracie Allen's (radio's Burns and Allen, I'll explain when your thirty) sense of comic timing, and Hail Mary full of Grace, a wish as much as a prayer for guidance upon your journey...

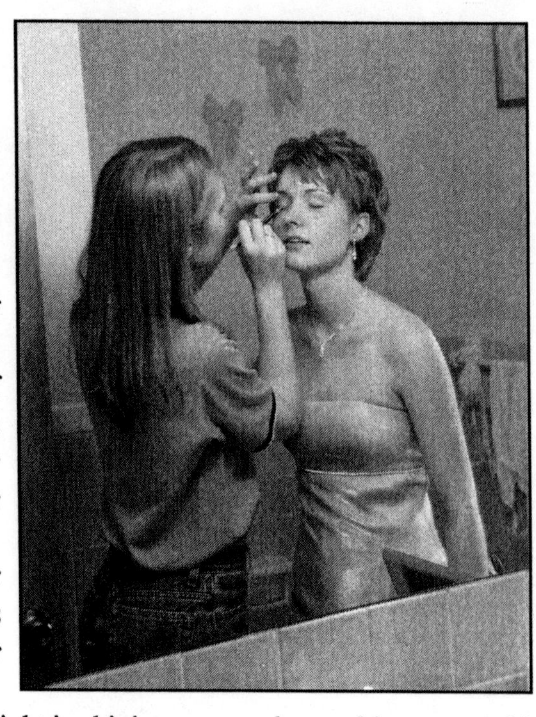

Close your eyes kiddo and lets make a wish together now.

I wish the knight in shining armor whose taking you to this prom sees the huge heart balancing between those too bare two shoulders. It is still a heart hunting for its heading, a heart with much yet to learn and much yet to share, but nevertheless a thing nearly fully grown.

I wish your older sister, who so tenderly now touches your make-up, can understand a part of her is also going off to the prom tonight. The part which sisters share always forever bonded into one living person. My wife and her sister (your mom) feel this bond ever more dearly today as you hook one open-toed, high-heel shoe upon your slender foot, and they cry. Tears flowing not from eyes but from unspoken bonds in blood.

I wish your classmates will celebrate this prom night and all its trappings, (cool blue gowns, clunky tall heels, and stiff tuxedoes with white-collared shirts) in confidence while showing caution. A senior prom is both a dressing up and a dressing down. It is a time when stiff tuxedos and tight gowns suggest an adult future…but the all-night pizza and video prom marathons afterwards warn how the future must be navigated from your raw teenage present.

But now I'm sounding like a dull uncle. And what I really wish is not dull at all. I wish, as your sister finishes the final make-up brush stroke, that you'll open your eyes and look in the mirror. And I wish what you see is your mother looking at you and her mother looking at her, and another mother looking at them… And on and on, deeper and deeper into the looking glass until the final bare-shouldered girl in the blue dress is you and them, the same person full of grace, a beginning and an end.

Open your eyes, Sara, and join them. They are all there, smiling… *—April 2001*

# Tales of the White Castle widower

I'm a White Castle widower. My wife is a closet "Castle Queen." She loves those greasy, onion-flavored sandwiches of the sack. And that's how she buys them—by the sack.

It's sacking our marriage. She's first in line when they open, and she often sneaks out late at night for a snack. At first I thought my rival was another man…but no cologne ever smelled so greasy.

I learned the greasy truth when her late night indiscretions became less than subtle.

"Honey, it's late. Why are you getting out of bed?"

"Go back to sleep, Charles. I'll just be a minute."

"But you're getting dressed. Where are you going at this time of night?"

"I…I just want to mail a letter."

"A letter? At two o'clock in the morning!"

"Yes, they're open 24 hours a day…"

"Huh? Who's open 24 hours? The post office? If that's so, then it'll be news to the postmaster general of the United States!"

"Uhh, no dear. Silly me, I meant to say the mailbox in front of the post office is open."

"So's the book drop at the public library! But normal people don't drop off books or mail letters at 2 a.m.!"

"Will you please just go back to sleep! I'll be home in about an hour."

"An hour! The Elizabethtown Post Office is just around the corner. What are you really up to?"

"If you must know…I have to go to Radcliff."

"Why Radcliff?"

"Radcliff? Err… they're faster there!"

"Honey, do you feel all right? You know, you've been acting mighty strange lately."

"Honestly, Charles, I just have this letter to…"

"How about that case of Pepto Bismol you bought? I can understand us needing a bottle. I might even believe we need two bottles, but an entire supermarket case? I call that mighty strange!"

"My stomach's been (burp) upset lately, Charles. It must be a bug. But I have to go now. Do you want anything to go?"

"From the post office?"

"Oh, I guess not."

"Listen. You're my wife. And if this is something you have to get out of your system then I won't stop you. But please, hurry home."

"I will, I will. They have a drive-through window now."

— *March 1983*

# Geese tale

Every winter my father tells the same story about geese freezing their feet. He first told me as we drove past a frozen pond back home. He pointed out geese flapping their wings and said, "The reason they can't fly off is, their feet are frozen to the ice."

Not a winter has gone by I haven't watched every lake and pond I've passed checking to see if the geese were frozen, trapped on earth. As a kid I made dad put a shovel (why a shovel, not an axe?) in the car so if we drove past a flock of frozen-footed geese, I could run down to the water and rescue them.

"Son, how would you do that?" he asked.

"I'd chip away at the ice and set them free."

My dad liked that. Before a car trip he'd always ask me to run get the shovel because it was cold and icy out and we might need it. I figure the shovel was really just his precaution in case the car slipped off the road. A shovel can come in handy when winter spins your wheels.

Looking back, I suppose the geese story spun out from how geese rotate their wings on cold winter days, drying their feathers and testing the wind.

On a cold day, on a bright frozen lake, it might appear birds indeed had frozen their feet. I suppose the old man laughed at his own joke more than once as we drove through town, a snow shovel in the back seat and my restless eyes searching for a safe take-off from the geese we'd pass.

Today I sit on the dock by Harmony Cove these winter mornings. The geese gather near the south end where the water almost never completely freezes. They swim round and round, stirring the cold water, ensuring an open circle in a cove of ice. Circling almost as if by instinct, spinning and chipping away at the frozen ice, clearing a lifeline to the future and spring.

These geese have become accustomed to my restless gaze. It is amazing what creatures can adapt to in the cold seasons of life. Even the winter sun's brilliant reflection off the show shovel I dutifully carry with me down to the dock, flashing, like the flash of some old Aegean warrior's shield, does not scatter the birds to flight.

I sit and watch them walk the ice. I sit, smile, and I miss my father. He sits 800 miles away back home in his SEARS TV recliner chair watching the weather channel. He keeps tab on me through the TV weather reports, telling me over the phone how Kentucky's weather was today and will be tomorrow. He is almost always right. And when he's not, I say he is anyway. It's my dime.

My father often corrects me and saying it's no thin dime allowing such a long-distance call. And I tell him he's right, absolutely right.

"So we'd better hang up," he says, and reluctantly we do.

But before we do, I always tell him the geese are flapping their wings down on the cove's ice, but can't take flight.

"Of course not son," he says back to me, so clearly I can hear him smile. "You know the problem, their feet are frozen. Do you still remember what to do?"

I sure do, Dad. I'll go get the shovel and chip the ice away.

*— February 2000*

# Remembering anniversaries

This spring I celebrate 25 years as a Villanova University graduate. Charles P. Spataro, class of 1975, editor of the literary magazine and...then what?

In the Villanova Alumni News you can write in and tell the folks what you've been doing since graduation. For me the answer is easy. "After college I drifted around for a while, finally hooking up with my fellow New Jersey legends and Italian buddies, Frankie Valli and the Four Seasons. For the next few years in tiny Jersey shore bars and fancy Long Island dinner clubs I sang backup on "Sherry," "Ronnie," "Big Girls Don't Cry," "Working My Way Back To You," and "Let's Hang On."

Most people think of "*Sherry, Sherry, Ba-A-by*" when they think of Frankie Valli. But that was just their first hit. The best, the very cathedral of falsetto vocals, came later in 1964 with "Rag Doll." Frankie's haunting, "*Ooo-Ooo-O-oo Rag Doll Ooo-I love you just the way you are...*" put the boys in the Rock 'n Roll Hall of Fame.

In an era when the Beatles owned the airwaves, these Jersey boys sang the East Coast Italian-American blues, and I sang along with them for three years after college. The only difference was I had to pay to get in.

When my falsetto voice gave out, I ended up in graduate school at Ball State University, and then a fella named Dr. Jim Owen (whose rich Alabaman speech is about as far away from a Jersey falsetto as you get) offered me a job in Elizabethtown. I have been here since 1978.

Around 1978 I fell in love with a dark-eyed girl who could sing all the high notes in "Sherry" and "Rag Doll." I still remember dating in places like the old Sonic on North Mulberry Street and at the Moo Dairy Queen on Dixie and at the Starlite Drive-in movie theater with my future Mrs. S. at my side. We'd be eating a dog at Sonic and Frankie Valli would come on over the radio of my stylish 1972 Ford Pinto. I'd turn up the sound and say, "Hey, back in Jersey, I used to sing with these guys."

"Yeah, and I dated Elvis," Mrs. S. would say.

"No, really I was in the backup band. Me and Frankie were just like this."

And I would hold up two fingers and Mrs. S. would squeeze some mustard over them and say, "put some relish on it…"

"No really, I sang backup," and to prove it I'd join in.

"*She's a Rag Doll, pretty Rag Doll. Such a pretty face should be dressed in lace.*"

"OOO-cough-ouch-@#*!" I just couldn't hit the high notes.

And instead of laughing at me (which wasn't all that hard to do with my voice cracking, my shirt, mouth and fingers covered in mustard), she'd turn the sound down low.

And then she'd sing falsetto, high, sweet like girls can do. And she knew all the words to "Rag Doll," knowing some of the words I'd even forgotten. She sang soft but steady in the voice I never had and at that very moment I knew I would marry her.

The wedding came in April 1980, 20 years ago. So this week I guess I have two anniversaries to remember. The day I left Jersey as a son of Villanova and the day I married the music I can still hear but not sing. *—April 2000*

# Welcome to the world, Carl

From my porch I see a jet crossing above the cove, plowing a billow in the sky. The sun is setting and my wife is talking on the phone in the kitchen, holding a bowl of brownie mix, stirring fifty strokes. Stirring with the phone balanced between her left shoulder and ear, she laughs and says in a baby talk-voice, "Hello, little Carl."

On the other end of the phone is her sister Tammy, the proud mom of our new nephew Carl. It sounds like Carl has had his first bath today. Water stands in a tub, swirling round. Both my wife and her sister are laughing. Tammy with her son on her hip, and Mrs. S. moving the brownie mix bowl to her hip, laughing, spinning a wooden spoon round and round.

I'm looking up as the jet's plume crosses two telephone lines in the yard. I'm imagining Baby Carl seeing his first jet, Baby Carl eating his first brownie, and Baby Carl catching his first fish. Such is the big world for a small boy to learn. Seeing me on the porch, my wife motions me to come to the phone, as she lifts the brownie mix bowl off her hip placing it on the kitchen counter.

Born in 2000, Carl's birthdays will count off the new century. When he turns one, so will the century. When he is ten, a decade will have gone past. Carl has quite a magical world to learn about. I'm thinking how lucky he is, lucky to be a millennium baby and lucky to have all the right numbers counting his take-offs and landings. Lucky, too, having the mother and the aunt he does. Just then a fish pops out of the cove, snapping at supper, and tasting the cold March oxygen. A dog barks, some geese honk, and the jet, silent as an icicle, grows into a long white chalk mark: going, going…gone.

Inside that jet there are people. Perhaps a flight attendant is carrying ice for someone's soft drink. A businessman is dozing, his hand wrapped around a half-empty cup of bourbon and cola. A young married couple is coming home from a honeymoon in Cancun and is sleeping, their sunburns just beginning to itch beneath the plane's stiff blanket. Everyone's safe, 30,000 feet above earth, and everyone is coming home.

All these things—the passing jet, the clinking brownie bowl, the fish gulping oxygen—all happen silently as icicles, melting softly as chalk dust. But this boy will not. Carl will come to know the jet, the brownie, and the gulping fish, as I know them. All in good time, baby Carl, all in good time.

But maybe, if the philosophers are correct and babies are born with infinite knowledge, then Carl knows all this already. Life may well be a falling, and a gradual forgetting of things self-evident at birth. I have held Carl, that warm, yawning, fleshy loaf with a boy's fingernails. Maybe he knows more than he's telling. Maybe his laughter I can hear over the phone is not mere instinctual newborn joy, but the calm understanding of an old soul. A soul that has already flown past the plume of every passenger jet in the sky.

He's a lucky boy, a soul just beginning to billow his mark. Stroke one of more than fifty in a round sweet bowl. Lucky boy. Lucky world. Have a good flight, little fish. *— March 2000*

# Grandma: a superstition for every circumstance

Last week I bought a suit. It must have made my old grandmother, who's been dead now for more than 25 years, turn over in her grave. Grandma used to say any time you bought a new suit it meant someone in the family was going to die. Granny used to say lots of things like that. She was an expert on curses and demons. She was from the old country. Well, actually, she lived near us in Northern New Jersey, but the geography sometimes got stretched for effect.

I don't believe in such superstitions. But standing in front of the three-sided mirror in Elizabethtown's downtown clothing store, a store that used to be a funeral home, I wondered if Granny wasn't somewhere behind the glass looking back, smiling.

The store clerks had never heard the old wives' tale linking death and a new suit. They had never met my grandmother. Granny had a million superstitions to guide your life. She told me never to look directly into a radio because then the person speaking could read your mind. If true, Ron Boone [a local radio personality] must really know how to keep a secret.

Granny lived with us for a time while I was a kid growing up. She protected me with her knowledge of the dark side. For example, she warned me never to use another person's pencil in school. Because, with another person's pencil, Granny said, I'd only write another person's thoughts. I remember in fifth grade breaking my point on purpose during spelling tests so the teacher would let me borrow her pencil.

Granny also didn't believe in opening an umbrella in the house. If you happened to be a kid who liked to play Batman jumping from the stair top using an open umbrella for a bat-parachute, then let me tell you the trouble you were in.

According to Granny the only way to break the curse of an umbrella was to wash it at midnight. But you had to use freshly cut onions and vinegar. Talk about crying yourself to sleep at night. But Grandma promised bad luck and bad spirits would haunt both the family and me unless I followed her rituals.

With Granny around, who needed Stephen King?

Granny's omens and curses could confuse you. A black cat was a good sign, not bad. What was bad, was an all-white creature, like a pure white bird or cat or horse. I remember once when TV's Lone Ranger came to our neighborhood for a promotional appearance. Seeing a black-masked man atop his pure white stallion, (handing out boxes of Tide detergent at the grocery store parking lot) well, it almost gave Grandmother a heart attack there and then.

Grandma could read and write English but pretended not to. Her many spell-breaking prayers and novenas seemed more powerful spoken in Italian. She spoke English only when she had to. She spoke Italian in all matters of the heart and mind. And she usually spoke her Italian in a low whisper. When she got really upset she looked like the Lost in Space robot (she was sort of built like it, too), waving her arms, whispering in Italian about warnings and danger.

I remember once she waved her arms and whispered up a storm over a birthday present. My folks had given me the novel, "Moby Dick," for my fourteenth birthday. Grandma's evil spirit detector blew a fuse.

"Grandma," I said, "I don't understand a word of Italian, so you don't need to whisper. You could shout and I still wouldn't understand!" And one of her robot-like claws grabbed my left ear and yanked. (Even today, during my fitting downtown, the store clerks noticed how my left ear is stretched bigger than the right.) Holding me by the ear she whispered something Italian to my mom. My mother whispered something Italian back. Then Granny let go of my ear and picked up my book and read in perfect English,

"'Moby Dick, the Great White Whale' by Mr. Troublemaker, Herman Melville. What kind of fish is this white fish? Is he a good fish?"

"I think he's not a fish at all," I said, rubbing the blood back into my ear. "I think the writer is making a metaphor."

"Met-a-four? Sure. What's he think he is, Casey Stengil? Don't use big words to your sick, old grandmother. And listen to what I say, a white fish is not to be trusted."

The funny thing is, I bet Mr. Melville would have liked my Grandmother.

Then there was the time I broke my arm. I was nine and I was poking around a construction site across the street. I slipped and fell down a deep hole. The ambulance (a white vehicle that my grandmother thought was Satan's chariot) came and took me to the emergency room. A doctor in a white mask (thank God Grandma stayed in the waiting room) set the bone. Later I heard the Doctor tell my mother it was a nasty break. He said there'd most likely be some pain tonight. Grandma and mother thanked him for doing his best, and then Grandma told the Doctor we'd (meaning she'd) take over from here.

That night I lay in bed unable to sleep because of the dull throbbing in my shoulder. Grandma paced outside my bedroom door. She wore these thick, heavy, black shoes, like the Frankenstein monster. I remember her shoes pacing past the one-inch opening of light under my door.

Finally, she crept into my bedroom carrying her big sewing scissors. With the pain in my arm, I figured stabbing me quickly was doing me a favor. But what she did was cut a huge chunk of hair off my head. And then she told me, "You sleep now little one. Your pain will soon pass away."

"How? What you gonna do Grandma?"

"I'm going across the street. I'm going to find where you fell and bury this hair with your pain. Grandma will be gone just a few minutes. When I come back you'll sleep."

I remember my shoulder bones mended slowly. But they did. Grandma would hold me in front of the bathroom mirror and show me how my hair was growing back. To her (and to me?) the new hair was proof of the healing bones. Every day we watched together in the mirror for the sure signs of healing.

Later that summer the Miller family moved into the new house across the street. Grandma had me take over some freshly baked bread, carrying it under my fully mended left arm. I always wondered if the Miller's knew that buried somewhere down in their basement, mixed among the cement and cinder blocks, Grandma had buried my pain.

So last week, standing in front of a three-way mirror I watched the clerks fit me for a new suit. And looking out from Grandma's eyes I thought about what she told me. How a new suit meant a death in the family. But maybe this was one time when Grandmother got it wrong.

Maybe a new suit doesn't forecast a new death so much as it helps to fondly remember someone who passed on long ago.
*— April 1999*

# Lean on me...

Have you ever watched an elderly couple stroll across a garden path and wonder if that will be you in 40 years?

No, not so much wonder as hope—hope you'll be like them, still together, still healthy enough (at 90 or 95), holding each other's elbow, supporting each other to bend (bending now a team sport which takes the combined skill of two) to smell the roses.

I saw such an endearing couple in a garden at New Harmony, Indiana, not long ago. The gentleman was helping his mate of many years walk the garden path. In a flash I saw the future in 40 years, my spouse holding onto me, both my arthritic knees shot, eyesight failing, my hearing fading as we walked the garden until my spouse said, "Let's get along home, you still have to finish your column."

I think what a marriage is, is this: two people who together help each other bend to smell the roses, who with hands stiff as crab's claws hold each other tight, reminding one another of the light in the gardens, gardens they have tended together. Pointing to birds high in trees singing songs they no longer hear, pausing as the man asks, "Isn't she a turtle dove?" And his wife, raising on her tiptoes as she has with him for nearly 70 years, whispers in his ear, "ho-cahoo-hoo" echoing a sound they once could hear.

She still makes up the bed early every day and he still complains that he wasn't done sleeping in it yet. She still lets all the neighbors' cats inside to eat and to play while he threatens to call the sheriff to come either take them or her (preferably BOTH) away. And at day's end as he stares at the tree, the one they planted when their child died, and tears fall down his wrinkled cheek, she, passing him a paper towel and a cup of tea, understands.

In fall they rake leaves together, noting how each year their pile is smaller but takes just as long to rake. A handyman now comes and finishes their yard. And when the handyman asks why he has him leave the pile they raked alone, the old man says, "We aren't done sleeping in it yet," and she laughs and sighs and tells the handyman to pay her husband no mind, because that is what he has—no mind left at all.

And after fall, the winter comes. More tea and honey comes home in the grocery bags these days. Less steak. He always asks her to buy thick, juicy steaks. And she grabs his arm and asks, "Whose teeth are you gonna use to chew with, old man?" and he says, "It was 70 years eating your leather cooking that wore my teeth out!" and she sighs (a sound that reminds him of a turtle dove's call?) and replaces the steaks, all but one, and he winks with pleasure at her concession.

In the parking lot the teen bag boy puts their plastic grocery bags into the trunk and the old man faces the boy, "Son, would you accept a tip from an old man?" The boy says, "Sure," and holds out his hand, expecting a dollar bill. The woman, squeezing the steering wheel with both hands, shakes her head and beeps the horn hoping to prevent a long speech on the decay of modern society given to the poor bag boy.

"Well, OK then, here's your tip. Marry for memory."

"Marry for what?"

"For memory. Long ago I used to be a young man like you. Can't recall any of it now. But see my wife in the car? She remembers it for me."

"Most peculiar thing," he says to his wife as she drives off in the Galaxy 500. "That boy held out his hand as if he wanted to shake with me. I don't remember all the young boys as being such strange fellows, do you?"

"That I don't know. But I do remember an old one who still is." *— September 2000*

# Mema and milestones

Today's column is a milestone for me. I am writing it to myself as sort of a note tucked away in a bottle to read 45 years from today. Lord willing, on that day I'll be a healthy 90-year-old former columnist. And I'll be looking back on a long and happy life. The big 9-0 is on my mind because our family is celebrating the 90th birthday of a beloved member. She's our Mema (mim-maw), my wife's grandmother. Mona Logsdon. You might remember her serving an ice cream sundae across the fountain counter at Boyd's Drugs. I want to say more than happy birthday to her, I want to say thank you for setting the mark. I am shooting for 90, too.

At 45 I've made it halfway. But that's not the milestone on my mind. Today marks my 365th column. I now have a prose picture for every day of a single calendar's year. That's a milestone. I probably have enough of a collection for a book. Or as Gerald Lush says, I've columns enough to make a decent fire for toasting some fine marshmallows. Ah, the tender words of an admiring editor. Mr. Lush has edited a good chunk of these epistles and he can testify they do add up to a lot, a lot of broken sentences and misspelled words. At about 1,000 words per column, well, perhaps Gerald deserves the first marshmallow.

It's funny, but as my family gathers celebrating Mema's 90 years I know these good folks are only part of my real family. Gerald Lush is also like family. Whoever you are reading this column now, you are also my family, even you, sitting at a Laundromat by the college. This paper smells of Tide and coffee stains from you and the two previous readers. (So, at twenty dollars a year why not subscribe already?) Together you all make up my family.

And you sir, waiting on that bench in Glendale. Your wife enjoys her antique shopping, doesn't she? I have been waiting on that same bench. I know the spot well. I know how the smell from The Whistle Stop's oven-baked bread turns the pages of this newspaper. You sir, and the smells of Glendale, are family to me.

You madam, sitting at J-Me and Company's beauty shop, I know you also. You sit calling out the paper's crossword inviting the hair stylists and their customers to help you finish the puzzle. You are all my family as well. Your cousin, and my dear wife, says the crossword puzzle is sometimes the only thing worth looking at in Gerald's newspaper. Occasionally, I'd have to agree. Tell me, isn't it a comforting thing to call out to family and friends for help solving a puzzle?

We have worked that puzzle and 364 others like it, side by side. We are relatives bonded by the blood of what we've shared together here in Hardin County and by what together we have written and read. Across many editions of many papers we've been celebrating something, all of us, together.

Mema's party makes me think of my own deceased grandparents. I wish they had left me a trail of 365 columns to remember them by. In a way they left their trail not with words but in blood, the blood of their children. My parents in turn left me marking their trail, carrying their hopes, dreams and memories forward. Childless, I write these columns like a bald and quite possible boring Hansel holding tight to his Gretel dropping bits of words instead of breadcrumbs as we go.

I know I'm not an Ernest Hemingway with these words. I'm probably closer to that other Ernest if you "Know what I mean, Vern?" But words often record real heartbeats no matter how unworthy the writer. Words can reveal the heart-held hopes of today, or of 45 years from today, preserving in spirit the true smell of bread on a breeze as a restaurant door swings open; a flash, a gust of wind, like blood; a memory trail…

When I write, when any essayist writes as I have written in these last 365 columns, we pray our word-thoughts become more than our thoughts alone. We hope we touch the thoughts of others, perhaps tracing common hopes, marking the shape-less dreams of this nameless family we all belong to. And somehow, not through personal genius but more by a given grace, these shapeless things take life in print. Not life as it truly is, blood to blood, but a life nevertheless.

Did I write well today? If someone sitting on a bench in Glendale puts down his paper and upon smelling bread on the wind, says "that is what I just read" then yes, I wrote well today. If the woman getting a cut and a color at the beauty shop pauses, paper in hand, before placing her knotted, wet-head inside the dryer and wonders, "has he been here?" then yes, I've written well today. Should a city councilman, tired from hours of talking, toss the minutes from his meeting in the trash but keep this paper to show his wife, then yes again. Yes to words written not by me but by all ourselves, by all our hearts, all our hopes, and all our graces.

So with today's column I have reached a milestone. Soon I'll be leaving my desk to attend a party for my much beloved 90-year-old Mema. Together we will celebrate certain trails left behind. She has left a daughter, who begot another daughter who became my wife. Blood to blood to blood. I honor all three lives today. All three are like candles on a cake, stories burning still.

I believe a life's story rests in these columns. If you are slightly more than a casual reader, you might agree. Should some niece or nephew want to discover who a bald and bad poet of an uncle was, 46 years from today (remember, Mema is my role model) perhaps there is a trail to follow. A prose trail in 365 columns. But like that grand Mema whom I honor this week, we are not finished yet. We are at a milestone, surely, and going on. *—February 1999*

# As Time Goes By—the kiss

*"You must remember this, a kiss is just a kiss..."*

These lyrics come from "As Time Goes By," an old song found in the classic movie "Casablanca." I can't hear the song and not think about the single most powerful kiss I'd ever received prior to meeting my Mrs.

Before coming to Kentucky I lived in Indianapolis for a while. I worked out of a downtown office. As a young and restless bachelor man, I took my lunch hour with sandwich in hand and wandered the city streets. Lunchtime in the city was when all the pretty office girls came out.

I called them office girls then, because I was nothing more than a pup myself, the ink not yet dry on my save-the-world master's degree. I remember the noon hour full of young secretaries and office workers in tall heels and short office suits pouring out from dull-shaped skyscrapers seeking a few moments in the fresh air and sunshine.

I walked from the memorial fountain to the farmer's market and back again watching their dresses swish in the summer's breeze and listening to the clip-clop of their designer shoes on sidewalk stone. Traffic hummed throughout downtown Indy as cabbies and delivery trucks whisked in and out making time.

I was single, owned two and a half suits, and had a business card in my wallet that said I worked for the Cooperative Extension. I was sort of a city-style 4-H agent. I took my job "oh-so-serious" waging a righteous war on inner city poverty. But every day at noon I put the war on hold to watch the civilian parade of long, sexy tanned legs dance an eternal strut to youth.

I remember one day vividly. It was May, 1977. The Derby down in Kentucky (where was that?) was over and the talk was about the upcoming Indy 500. I dedicatedly was following two very thin legs that hurried past. They were wonderfully connected to a tight, yellow mini skirt at the top and a matching bare-toed sandal in a killer stiletto heel at rock bottom.

It was a busy business day. Hectic traffic rushed passed me and these yellow mini-skirted legs. She came to a street corner and rather than wait for traffic she flew across like a sprinter. I stopped at the corner watching her race away.

And suddenly a kid, a wonderful broken-tooth kid, (she couldn't have been eight) shot past me at the street corner. From behind I heard her mother call out "Regina…wait!" But Regina ran past me and into the street.

Now I have to explain what happened. Don't forget I am really drooling after the skinny legs, yellow mini skirt, and high heels, but then this happened. Regina rushed past me, and her mom cried, "Wait!" So I grabbed Regina by her right arm, which brushed by me as a racer's arm pumps for speed.

Don't ask me why I grabbed her. It was a busy street. The kid was gonna be hit by a cab for certain. But I think maybe I grabbed her because if I stopped her from getting killed then I'd have at least another 2.1 seconds of watching my yellow mini skirt goddess…

Nevertheless I grabbed her. And she was going so wild and fast that she pulled me one step off of the curb. I held onto her and sort of swirled her in a circle like the ballet dancers do on stage. Off into the air and back again. It's that swirl I remember most, more than the yellow mini-skirt. Go figure.

Then a cabby hit his brakes and everybody turned and suddenly the mom was there. Regina started crying and I saw the mom had on moccasins. Funny, I've never forgotten the mother's moccasins. They were the kind with little tiny pink and aqua green beads. It was like the mother was an ex-hippie or maybe a genuine American Indian, I don't know.

"Say thank you to the nice man," the mother said. (Nice man, wasn't I the sex pervert ogling a yellow mini skirt?) Regina looked down at her sneakers, took two confident steps forward, and kissed my cheek.

Well, I wasn't expecting that. I didn't want any little girl kissing me on Market Street in downtown Indianapolis. I didn't want to know this elegant, dark-haired mother in moccasins or her broken-toothed daughter. It was lunch hour, I had on one of my famous suits (from the collection of two and a half), and I wanted to be girl watching, not getting involved in other people's lives.

But it all happened so fast.

"Son, I guess you just about saved that little girl's life," said a bald, tourist-type guy. You know the kind, Bermuda shorts, brown knee socks, and sandals. He had a camera around his neck and was holding the hand of what could only be his wife. (Same socks, same sandals.) The wife was smiling at me teary-eyed, dripping something from her nose onto her loudly colored Indy 500 T-shirt.

The camera guy patted me on the back as Regina's mother swept her daughter away. Regina looked back at me as she got dragged off. You remember Natalie Wood in "The Miracle on 42nd Street"? That's what she looked like: beautiful, thoughtful, eight years old, and all the world's wisdom in two big brown eyes. And she was quite perfectly alive.

Well, I've been married now for nearly twenty years. Mrs. Spataro, well, she's everything to me. It is in her eyes that I have come to see the world. I love her more than it is possible to say. And as it turns out we never could have kids. The doctors have complicated explanations for why but I never really understood them much. You know doctors, they say things as clearly as they can...but sometimes it doesn't add up to much of anything. I figure I must have worn those two and half suits too damn tight is all...

Sometimes I think back on that day in Indianapolis, and I wonder how Regina turned out, after all. I wonder what my own daughter would have looked like? If she would have resembled the beautiful Mrs. Spataro the way Regina favored her own dark-eyed mom…

And I wonder why I was put there on that street corner in Indianapolis on that afternoon in May? Being childless I can count on my fingers the number of kisses a kid has given me. Maybe saving that kid's life was enough reason for being in Indy that spring? Anyway, how did the kid know to kiss me and not to just shake my hand?

Like I said I don't understand much. But watching a late night rerun of Casablanca this weekend at Harmony Cove, I have a notion. I suspect I didn't really save that kid's life at all. Looking back on it now, I think maybe, just maybe, she ended up saving mine?

*"A case of do or die. The fundamental things apply as time goes by."* —*April 1998*

## Real men don't do aerobics

Together my wife and I joined an athletic club. Nice place. A bit expensive, a touch too narcissistic, and perhaps it leans on being downright faddish—but the employees are friendly so we joined.

The place has most of what a health club should have. There are weights, universal exercise machines, nautilus equipment, and a jogging track. A snack bar features a large screen TV along with an assortment of food items (which will help put back on those extra pounds you just sweated off).

Tanning beds and tanning booths promise to keep some members brown while a delicious coed Jacuzzi succeeds in keeping all members in bliss. And like I said, the employees are friendly; so what's not to join?

Up on the club's second floor is its jogging track. That's where I hang out. My wife spends time both on the track and on the aerobic exercise floor. This brightly lit, colorfully decorated aerobics area rests (odd choice of word) in the center of the jogging circle. The result is that as I jog I can observe the women "doing" aerobics.

Except it's not just women. Some men "aerobicise" in center stage as well. I've had the opportunity to study the performance of both women and men engaged in aerobics and one thing seems certain—real men don't do aerobics.

I know what the health consultants will say, "Sure men can do aerobics. It's basic cardiovascular recreation. It's fun. It's gender-compatible to both guys and gals, and like wow, man, this is the 1980s for sure."

True. But men look silly doing aerobics. I'm not sure why they do. Women don't. Women look wonderful—more than wonderful. They look natural. They can even look elegant like a Jane Fonda or a Victoria Principal—but not the guys.

Jogging around the women (and one or two guys) the other day I tried to reason out why men look so dumb doing aerobics. I don't want to say something cute like gals look better in leotards because there's more to it than that.

I think it has something to do with the movement—something in the gestures, the actual mechanics of dance routines. Those bends, tucks, stretches and curls are, well, feminine.

Let me say it another way. When I watch Olympic gymnasts perform, I marvel at the excellence of both men and women. And yet even to my untrained eye I see a celebration of different types of physical excellence. Mary Lou Retton does not "do" what Bart Conner "does." Each athlete is unique, each is a champion, but their bodies express grace and strength in distinctly different manners of motion. Female. Male.

So too, I'd argue, is the case of tennis players. The baseline game played by tennis greats Chris Evert and Jimmy Connors are pure poetry in motion. They play the same game and yet they celebrate it with different movements, different gestures, different "poems" in motion.

At the athletic club, wonderfully fit and exclusively feline employees lead the aerobic workouts. And the motions, the steps, the very architecture of each routine are, consciously or subconsciously, feminine and wonderfully so. When men join in they most certainly benefit from the cardiovascular activity—but they look dumb in the doing, dumb because the men are forced to mirror female-type motions.

I know this may all be a matter of opinion. My view is that real men don't do aerobics, plain and simple. And if anyone cares to argue the point, they can find me in the snack bar most every lunch hour...eating my quiche. *— November 1984*

# Red sports car envy is all-consuming

I'm fighting a losing battle with my wife and oh, how I'm suffering. You husbands out there will recognize my pain. Chances are you too have suffered as I suffer now. I hope not—I hope this never happens to anyone.

You see, my wife wants to buy a car.

Not any car, mind you, but a brand new, factory-fresh showroom automobile, the kind that says "one" on the mileage meter. A car with its sales sticker still arrogantly pasted on its side window.

She means business, too. It's a Pontiac Fiero she wants. A Pontiac Fiero—a low-sitting, flame red, two-seated, tire-burning, gas-guzzling sports car.

She first saw "her" Fiero on the corner of Dixie and Miles. Hardin Motors has it sitting there looking like a sleek red dagger waiting to stab out the heart of every female passing by.

Every time we pass by, my wife takes a long, long look. Then I count silently to myself (1,001--1,002--1,003) and she says, "Chuck, I want that car."

Every time we pass that darn intersection it's the same thing. (1,001--2--3) "Chuck, I want that car."

It's gotten to the point that I avoid Dixie and Miles. I reroute our travel with 30-minute detours just to avoid that darn flame-red Fiero. But then we'll pass one on the road (1--2--3) "Chuck, I want that car."

I partly have myself to blame. One morning after church, I let my wife talk me into pulling into the Hardin Motors lot. I never should have, but I did. Then I let her get out; she ran straight for the Fiero.

It took four salesmen and one crowbar to pry her off the car.

Twice now she's disappeared from the house and twice I've found her at Hardin Motors. The salespeople there just open the door when they see her coming. Then they call me to come and fetch her.

I say, "Hi, honey."

She says, "Chuck, I want this car."

Other times we sit at home and rationally discuss the topic of buying a car.

I say, "Maybe we should shop around a little."

She says, "Chuck, I want this car."

I say, "How does it do on gas?"

She says, "I want THAT car."

I say, "Is it easy to drive?"

She says, "Drive, shmive. Read my lips. I want that car."

The Fiero is a beauty. It's America's only mid-engine production car. The Pontiac people are quick to point out it was No. 1 in a recent government safety study.

All of that doesn't really matter. According to my wife, the Fiero and her were made for each other. And she doesn't want any Fiero, she wants that one. The one on the corner of Dixie and Miles. The one we pass by every day.

I say, "Let's not rush into this."

She says, "I want that car."
I say, "We'd better ask about its maintenance record."
She says, "I want that car."
I say, "What does Consumer Reports have to say?"
She says, "It says that Mrs. Spataro wants that car."
I say, "It's expensive."
She says, "You only live once."
I say, "Wouldn't you really rather have a Buick?"
She says, "No, I want that car."
I say, "At Ford, Quality is Job One."
She says, "But I want that car."
I say, "Renault is the one to watch."
She says, "I want that car."
I say, "Dodge is America's Driving Machine."
She says, "I want that car."

I'm fighting a losing battle with my wife. I've got many good reasons, good slogans, good excuses not to buy her new car, but they don't seem to matter.

You see, *she wants that car.* — *October 1984*

# Abbey Road album

If you look in the upper left-hand corner of the Beatles' Abbey Road album you'll see a white Volkswagen Beetle. It's mine. Or at least that's my story, and I have two or three buddies who'll back me up, or I think they would if I knew where they all went off to after we graduated from Villanova University and joined the real work-a-day world.

I actually did drive a white Beetle Bug around Villanova all those many years ago. She was the only car my pals and me had amongst us. This was years ago, way back before John, Paul, George, and Ringo split, back as George puts it "*long time ago when we was fab.*" Back in those days we'd slap on our Old Spice and High Karate cologne, pile into Snowball (as we called her) and drive. In twenty minutes we'd be in downtown Philadelphia as "*she came in through the bathroom window*" screamed out the Bug's permanently busted, half-open driver's side window and the smell of Philly cheese steaks drifted in.

Even then, I always figured to tell my children the white Volkswagen Beetle on the Abbey Road album was mine. How, one summer I took all overseas study courses and met up with the Fab Four outside their studio. And how Ringo really was funny and how Yoko really was shy and a great cook. And what an amazing time we all had. Or maybe it was just me who was, A-mazed.

I always figured I'd tell my son (who we'd call Ringo, because with my genes, he was never gonna be a dreamboat like Paul) how sweet smelling the London streets were. How it swung like a pendulum do. And my baby girl, well, my wife could name her but I'd always call her, Abbey Roads, and I'd balance little Abbey on my knee and show her the white Bug and say, "That's Daddy's car. It's the car in the garage right now. It's the car I met your mommy in."

"Really, Daddy?"

"Why sure little Abbey. That's the car I let Paul borrow whenever he wanted to run out for some shoes or cigarettes."

"He's barefoot in the picture Daddy. Why is he barefoot?"

"Cause Paul and your Daddy had just finished playing basketball. Paul's feet were blistered. Paul had a tough voice but tender feet. Now if you don't believe me, Abbey Dear, you go ask your mommy if she remembers it that way..."

And my wife would laugh and say something about all she remembers for sure is how small that white Bug was, and how the Philadelphia winter wind would rip right through that busted window. And how I kept a big Villanova football blanket in the back seat. A thick, cuddly sweet, Villanova blue and white blanket.

Well, I never did get to have a Ringo or an Abbey Roads. But like the song says, "*in the end the love you take is equal to the love you make.*" After I moved to Kentucky I met a kind and gentle woman who took me in off the street and married me. We have a cat named Abbey, who's plenty sweet and before she sleeps I swear she purrs like an air-cooled engine.

And I am looking real hard these days at buying a new car. There's this spanking new white Beetle in a lot just down Dixie Highway that sure brings back memories. The way its front grill smiles, a sort of benign smile, reminds me of my old pal Ringo.

At least that's my story and I'm sticking to it.

— *October 2000*

# Knee pain's a strain

There's nothing quite so painful as a knee injury. If you don't believe me, just ask my wife. Ever since I hurt my knee—it's been absolutely killing her.

Mrs. S. and I used to go to work together in the mornings. That was before my knee died. Now, I stay home like a pig in a poke while she brings home the bacon.

My life is a simple one. She brings me breakfast in bed and kisses me goodbye. Then I eat and watch TV. After a while, I fix a snack and take a short nap. Next I find something to munch on and read the papers. Or I doze. In all, I gradually manage to wreck the house.

Wrecking the house, as any wife can explain, is what husbands do while "convalescing" from illness at home. It's not as if I mean to mess up the place on purpose—I can't help it. I can't take time to straighten my mess because of the pain (that's BOTP, for short) in my knee.

BOTP (because of the pain, remember?) I have to pace myself. I'm able to struggle into the bathroom for a shower and a shave, but the soggy towels and hairy sink bowl have to wait.

In order to keep up my ebbing strength, somehow I limp into the kitchen for a sandwich and a bowl of soup. But the dishes remain. And after I read the morning paper, I'm usually too drained to fold it up again. Because of the pain.

So I collapse back into bed, and hope Mrs. S. comes home soon for her lunch. Not that she'll have time to eat anything. Once she cleans the house, she wraps my knee in a special ice pack. I'd apply the pack myself, but because of the pain, I can't touch my knee.

After she leaves to return for work, I sometimes feel a little guilty. But I've found it passes if I take a nice long nap. Waking refreshed, I buckle down to help out around the house. I do this by making Mrs. S. some "to do" lists.

I write out reminders for her "to do" the dirty clothes, "to do" the food shopping, and "to do" some more ironing. Since I'm not going to work it's an ideal time for me to help Mrs. S. get better organized around the house.

When she arrives home after a hard day at the office, we chat. "How was your day?" she asks.

"Don't ask," I answer. "It was as good as can be expected. I still keep passing out because of the pain." I always try and zing her with a few BOTPs before I wince, moan, and sigh. "How…(quiver, tears dripping from my eyes) how was your day, dear?"

By then I've got her so snowed that she forgets the question and rushes to my side, saying, "Poor baby, can I do anything?"

That's when I hit her with the "to do" list. "No, (cough, grab for the knee but stop short of touching it BOTP) I'll be OK now that you're home. I did manage to jot down a few things for you."

She reads: "Buy magazines. Get another case of Coors and barbecue chips. Pick up this week's TV Guide. Bake a chocolate cake and leave by bedside. Change sheets."

"Change the sheets?" she questions. "I just put those sheets on yesterday."

"I know you did, and I appreciate your doing that," I answer. "But today as I was finishing the pancakes you brought me for breakfast I must have spilled the syrup."

"How could you!"

"I think my knee was throbbing because of the pain and its vibrations shook the bottle off the tray. If it's too much bother we could let it wait. But it spilled mostly on your side of the bed."

"You win, I'll change the sheets."

Just then the phone rang. I made a pathetic attempt to answer it as Mrs. S. still steamed over the dirty sheets.

"Don't get up," she said. "You'll only hurt yourself."

She walked into the living room and answered the phone. "Hello. Oh hello mother. No, I don't think I can come over and visit you tonight."

There was a pause, and then with her voice aimed in my direction she said, "It's because of the pain." *—July 1982*

# The big leap starts with a few big hurdles

I'm trying to get married and there are many obstacles to overcome. Since locating a volunteer willing to serve as the bride, the entire process has become so complicated.

A few of the complications I knew about. These are the unimportant things like the price of gold rings, the price of new housing, the price of food, the price of fuel, the price of...well, you know about these things too. I considered such matters only a minor nuisance for the truly creative mind. But oh, never did I comprehend the real obstacles of getting married.

Like choosing a tuxedo. What you see is not always what you get. A formalwear catalog may show a tall, slim man dressed in a wonderful gray tux. That tux may soon become a funny black and white polka-dot suit on a confused columnist.

"Why is that suit polka-dotted?" I ask, glancing back at the beautiful catalog.

"The outfit looks gray from a distance, sir. Just be sure to hold your ceremony out on a football field. Guests may sit in the bleachers as the wedding party trots out on the 50-yard line. The numbers for your backs are provided at no extra cost."

Pre-wedding gifts are another problem. Already thousands of crockpots are being airmailed my way from doting relatives. However, no one actually had to go out and BUY these gifts. I have learned that 20,000 pots were labeled back in 1971, "For Wedding Gifts Only, Pass It On." The same boxes are shipped to all weddings in America.

The post office stacks the slow cookers in a warehouse just outside Elizabethtown. Lately a new problem has come up. We had a sudden rush of Mr. Coffee machines (my sentimental family always loved Joe DiMaggio). These are stored in the Knights of Columbus hall.

Then there is the matter of my new social conscience. As a happy-go-lucky single man, my counsel was not sought in local civic matters. Since the engagement, I must have become a much wiser man. Now my judgment (and dues) are in great demand in the many civic and social organizations of the community. Vive la matrimony.

My auto insurance agent has called several times. He does not consider me so wise. In fact, he wants me to weigh the serious responsibilities of marriage before acting. He urges me not to rush into anything. He asks me to be certain—before I file for the reduced rates a married man earns.

How my new wife improves my driving ability I'm not sure yet. She improves my character perhaps? She gives me a friend with whom to share decisions, but my driving? Maybe the auto insurance folks figure a man's reflexes improve after marriage. If so, I hope my tennis game also gets better.

Maybe a man's writing also improves after marriage? Maybe then columnists go on to become novelists, presidents, and astronauts. Maybe all the complications are worth it. After all, the worst that can happen is I'll open an outlet store for crockpots and coffee machines. *—January 1980*

# The shark's in perilous waters during tennis

One way we learn to grow is through the two-sided, give-and-take relationship, that, for want of a better word (but finding none), we call love.

I agree with Woody Allen's analysis of love. In his Academy Award-winning film, "Annie Hall," Woody states, "Love is like a shark." Allen explains to his lover Annie, played by Diane Keaton, exactly how love is like a shark.

It seems that sharks have to move forward or else they die. Somehow they take in oxygen as water passes across their body during forward motion. No forward motion…dead shark.

Love, so concludes Allen, is like a shark because love also must move forward. It must progress. In order for a relationship to remain healthy, it must take in new things. The forward movement among people that allows them to grow is oftentimes slow. It is oftentimes non-existent. It is called love.

By people in love I include all possibilities: mother-daughter, father-son, neighbor-neighbor, and husband-wife. As an example of what learning to grow (love) means in the everyday world, I can use my best friend, lover, and, since she'll be reading this I should quickly add, wife.

Recently we decided to add some forward progress to our marriage. We wanted to learn something together. Something fun. Something we could continue to progress at for the rest of our lives together. Coincidentally, it was July, the time of tennis' greatest championship, Wimbledon.

We both enjoyed watching tennis on TV. Tennis looked healthy, social, and promised to be an activity we could grow old together doing. Neither of us knew much about the game, but we decided to give it a go.

The "go" proved to be hard going at first. We found ourselves to be two very different people when it came to tennis love. I'm a bit of an athlete, having played basketball all my life. (When I come back in another life, I plan to come back as Bob Cousy). My wife, on the other hand, is the classic non-athlete.

So we had to be patient with each other and our different approaches to tennis (as in menace) love. I had natural eye-hand coordination. So it took me a while to realize that even a talented (read in here sexy, rhythmical, graceful) dancer like my wife needed to learn basic motor skills like a beginner.

I, on the other hand, had been blessed with two dead knees for all my basketball antics. My wife had to learn to remind and to coax my petrified knees to bend. We helped each other. I empathized with her eye-hand frustrations and she sympathized with the dead spot where my knees used to be.

We were (and still are) quite a sight on the tennis courts. I shout, "Think!" as she aims for the ball while she says a quick prayer each time I call upon a knee to bend. In all of this there exists a tenderness and a respect for the strengths and weaknesses we share.

This tenderness is not so trite a matter as it may seem. Tennis, and perhaps marriage in general, is a sport that can cause cruel and abusive behavior among its participants. A joke goes like this: What do you call it when a married couple plays tennis doubles? Answer…divorce!

But, so far at least, this has not been our experience—quite the contrary. We are sharing our forward progress in this sport. My wife has proven to be the one with the better form. (I could have told you that. I "luv" her in tennis shorts.) But I have the more powerful, if not somewhat awkward, style of stroking the ball.

She helps me with my form (bend those knees), and I encourage her to hit with more (use those dancer's hips) power. All the while we keep the Woody Allen shark in mind as a good metaphor for our loving, growing relationship.

If one of us gets impatient or too demanding, then that person is quickly calmed down with the reminder, "Honey, I think you're killing the shark." *—August 1983*

# Cello's strains a reminder of own wedding

I like the shape and sound of the word, cello.

Cello is a word that looks like the thing it is. If you stand the "c" on top and stack the e-l-l-o underneath, you pretty much have a big fiddle. But, by miss-labeling this string instrument "a fiddle," I just revealed my ignorance about classical music in general and cellos in particular.

And yet, a cello has been playing in the back of my mind for 19 years. Not some anonymous cello, but a specific one. Nineteen years ago this very Sunday, Bonnie Avery, the former Elizabethtown resident and long-time supporter of the Hardin County arts, played the cello at my wedding.

A few weeks ago Bonnie was in town performing in an ECC Home for the Arts concert at the Presbyterian Church out on Pear Orchard Road. What a beautiful place. The light alone in this church as it filters through those sacred stained-glass windows is awe-inspiring. The way this church community relocated from downtown to Ring Road while maintaining in the new building an architectural reminder of their former home, is a sign of their respect for both time and tradition.

My wife and I both attended the Bonnie Avery concert. We hadn't seen Sam Avery or his wife for many years. Sam still had his red beard, though now flushed through in silver. Bonnie had short hair, a wonderful surprise from the long, dark locks I remembered. And she still had the grace, that certain honesty, which I've noticed often accompanies those devoted to classical music. I believe this has something to do with a musician's unique sense of timing.

Mrs. Spataro and I took our seats, joining a fine crowd gathered to hear the cello and piano concert. Bonnie's cello played off to our right, just as it had 19 years ago as Joella and I took our wedding vows at St. James Catholic Church. As the recital unfolded, I wondered if this cello, this wonderfully crafted mirror to the human heart, was in fact the exact same musical instrument Bonnie cradled in St. James Church almost two decades ago?

My recollections of that day, April 11, 1980, are a soft blur. All I really remember for sure is Father Bill Martin wore black and Joella wore white. And I remember looking out into the eyes of about 100 guests. They all seemed so happy and somewhat surprised. My older brother, the best man, told me they were surprised because they all wondered how such an ugly guy could catch such a classy bride?

I vaguely recall stumbling through a traditional Catholic service. And I vaguely recall more than a few of my colleagues from Elizabethtown Community College turning out in force to see if Joella would finally come to her senses and back out. She didn't. And I do clearly recall the cello music, soft and heartfelt, filling the church like the sound candlelight would make. Bonnie Avery was the artist making that music glow, playing somewhere to our right.

During intermission at Bonnie's recent concert, I asked Sam to point out his children. Sam said their kids smelled "a big geezer reunion" of old Hardin County friends about to happen, so they wisely chose not to come along. I was about to make a joke about how the kids could have stood in the rear of the church, fists waving, shouting, "Yo Yo! Mom!" But luckily, several other "long-lost geezer friends" took Sam away, and the worst pun in the history of classical music mercifully slipped into oblivion.

There was something very mind focusing about the recital that day. Bonnie's cello became a personal clock allowing me to mark the time I'd traveled since I had last heard her play. Instead of using a "tick-tock," this cello clock measured time with a bow drawn back and forth across four strings. Each passing bow took me back in time.

In my mind's eye I hadn't changed a bit in these last 19 years. But if that were true, then why was my own once red beard even more silver-streaked than Sam's? I guess Rome really does burn while we just fiddle away the time. But sitting there wrapped inside the music, time slowed down enough for me to take a second peek. I saw our first apartment right down the road at Pear Orchard Estates. If you pressed your nose to the window, you could almost see Freeman Lake.

Now twenty years later we live smack dab in front of a lake at Harmony Cove.

As Bonnie played more time passed on. I remembered friends we'd gained and lost. I counted out the nearly twenty years Joella and I had worked together at Elizabethtown Community College as husband and wife. Once back in the early 1980's we became the state's first husband and wife co-coaches of an intercollegiate women's basketball team. Funny the things you do when you're young?

As Bonnie's bow framed a long, slow note, she tenderly wrapping herself around the cello as if needing the instrument's physical contact to produce a proper tone, I turned to reach for Joella's hand. And, although to my eyes my wife has managed to become a friend to time's passing, I noticed something. With her free hand Joella wistfully brushed through her own shortened hair.

And Bonnie played, holding close to one long, low note.

Later, after the recital, we met Bonnie at the reception line. She and Joella both giggled like teenage schoolgirls over their shortened hair. And I said, "At least you two still have hair to cut short!"

Bonnie told us she fondly remembered playing at our wedding. "Good times long ago," she said, touching her hair. I asked Bonnie if she still used the same cello she played at our wedding? And Bonnie smiled, "No. I just recently upgraded. This is a much better instrument, capable of producing so much more. And it's older!"

Maybe it's true what they say: The older the fiddle, the finer the tune. *— March 1999*

# Those starry eyes

I never wrote about the girl on the motorcycle. She has been in my mind for more than five years now—but I never could get her story to work out right.

As a columnist you sit at a typewriter coaxing from the keys the best work you can. In my short five years of writing I've tried the motorcycle story at least a dozen times. Never got the thing right.

So here goes, because right or not—some stories deserve to be told…

I never even met her. She was only some young kid I passed on the way to my first day and my first column for "The News-Enterprise." A red light caught me at a corner and out my car window I saw her waiting for the morning school bus.

She had thick, shaggy hair that reminded me of Loretta Lynn. And she had these two, deep brown, 8-year-old eyes that could shoot stars when she smiled.

Only, she didn't smile often. She stood off away from the rest of the bus kids and stared down at her "Star Wars" lunch pail. Every morning when I passed her I thought, "Gee that kid needs to get more sleep." She looked—well, she looked like a pretty little coal miner's daughter with the weight of the world on her shoulders.

That's all I really knew about her—a cute kid at a bus stop with stars for eyes. Not much for a column. Not much until the Saturday I saw her on the motorcycle. Since that day I'll bet not a month has gone by that I have not thought of her starry, starry eyes.

It was on a hot, muggy Saturday I saw her daddy (same Loretta Lynn face, same starry eyes) carrying the girl to his motorcycle. She was too weak to walk. She was dressed in one of her father's work T-shirts—a faded, black shirt which completely swallowed her like the evening sky.

I don't know any of the rest of this for a fact, but somehow I could sense the girl was dying. I don't think she could breathe very well. I believe her daddy took her on motorcycle rides when the weather got muggy. A motorcycle ride would push the wind around her shaggy, dark hair and into those tiny lungs.

That daddy was a good man. I only saw him the one time—but once was enough. He carried his star child to a spot near the motorbike. He joked with her while fastening her crash helmet. I saw her smile at some silly joke and her smile shot with the speed of light across the street into my car and lit up my dashboard.

When she smiled those eyes did shine like stars. It was clear she loved her daddy, loved how he pampered her with the motorcycle rides they enjoyed together.

I remember she was too weak to ride behind her father on the bike, so he cradled her in one arm to his chest as the bike punched forward in front of my car. The girl stretched up and kissed her daddy as they rode off.

That's it. That's all I saw of the girl on the motorcycle. Just a memory five years old—about as old as these columns of mine. Time to stop trying to get the story right. Time to let those two bright eyes wrapped up in a black T-shirt fade now...
*— July 1986*

## *Chapter Two*

# A Season to Celebrate

# Clydesdale carol

Although my friends remind me it's bad ecology, a fire hazard, and unhealthy for allergies, the Mrs. and I go to a tree farm and cut down a live Christmas tree every Yuletide.

We do it this way because, despite bad ecology, the risk of fire and runny noses, the tree farm is an astoundingly beautiful place. We go to a hill near a creek not far from Harmony Cove. Above the creek scattered on a slope crusted in ice are the trees, growing green in almost perfect rows. Below the creek is a pasture where draft horses graze quietly as it snows.

We go as much to see the horses grazing as for the trees. These perfect, thick-limbed giants seem to guard the evergreens

with mammoth hooves, round as snowmen heads, clawing at the frozen ground. They're fenced in nearly 100 yards away but watch our every move. They breathe white clouds into the night air from their moist, round nostrils. My wife says these gentle giants look like the Budweiser Clydesdales on Christmas break.

As we climb the hill, passing Christmas trees not quite ripe for cutting, the horses are always in sight. We pick our tree by a simple system. My wife walks to a tree and points. If one puffing, white-breathed behemoth in the field below shakes his mane in the negative, we walk on. At another tree further up we point again, and when the lead horse nods up and down, we cut.

Then we pay the proprietors and drag our tree down to the truck, passing baby trees already growing for next year. Halfway down the hill is a dark ring where every year they burn a bonfire late on Christmas Eve. Whole trees (cut and ordered but never picked up) burn like skeletons. This fire, fed with scraps of evergreen limbs and sawed off Christmas tree bottoms, can be seen for miles.

On Christmas Eve I return to the tree farm for this bonfire. I park my truck in the field below and wait for the hillside to glow. The proprietors sell trees clear through 9 p.m. on Christmas Eve. But as darkness settles in and the winter chill rolls down the hill they give away as many as they sell.

I go alone to the bonfire because, as Mrs. Spataro says, “How can I get ready for Christmas with you always prancing around underfoot!” And so, I drive my truck back to the tree farm and sit alone listening as a local radio station tells the time and temperature. I sing along to Christmas carols and wait.

Sipping hot coffee (sweetened with Maker’s Mark) I picture Mrs. Spataro wrapping presents back at Harmony Cove. Around 8:45 p.m., late for any business to still be open on Christmas Eve, they dig a trench around the by-now huge scrap pile of tree stumps and broken evergreen branches. After a red gasoline can sprinkles the ground, they torch the pile.

At first the orange glow hurts my eyes and seeing two fires I blink. Shutting the truck’s radio I roll down my window pouring out the remains of my Christmas cheer. The bonfire crackles in the cold. I always wait until everyone’s gone, staying to be alone with the burning fire of dying trees in whose light next year's seedlings grow.

Then, with just the wind's stillness, I realize I'm not alone. Somehow freed from their pasture, two horses approach the fire. They break the silent night with somber neighs. A joker, I call back at them, "Fall on Your Knees…Oh Hear the Horses Call."

Four moist eyes glow like red coals blinking open and closed. Once again the lead horse cries crossly in the night. He doesn't appreciate my spiked breath and brazen attitude in this holy place. I nod to him my apology. And the whole world seems there on that hillside waiting within a Clydesdale's call…

*— December 2000*

## Manger tonight

With my own eyes what do I see?

I see a black sky above the cold lake. I see an island across Harmony Cove, with a floodlight and an electric star hanging from a bare tree. So lights the manger we used last week for our live nativity scene. Looking out my window, I see them now.

Since holding our nativity, I've watched children come to play in the manger. They laugh at doing something naughty, being there. One giggling boy raises his hands, priest-like, giving benediction. Yet, each child looks so innocent standing there, nothing sacrilegious crosses my mind.

I've seen wild ducks huddling in the manger, hunkering down to the straw. A raw wind blows water in black sheets off the cove. These ducks chatter as they fight to stay dry. Perhaps it's a losing battle, staying dry, but a storm's just so much water off a duck's back. And even a makeshift manger gives us ducks some comfort.

I have seen that manger's star shimmer in the wind. It's a huge star, connected to the mainland by a thin cord, hung there by my neighbor. He's a kind man you'd love to meet. So the wind howls. So the rain blows. The star lights up and shivers, but survives. It is there now, trembling amongst the three trees on Christmas Island.

I wonder how many passers-by have seen the island's trees? Three trees, standing there like crosses on a hill. The manger is anchored to these trees. Anchored by rope and with nails hammered into wood. It's a make-do shelter, nothing more. But it will do. It has done and it will do.

And as night falls I see my neighbor plug in an extension cord. So connects a fragile line of current that crosses the cove and lights the star above the trees.

No one is in the manger tonight, or not that I can see. But sight plays funny tricks on my old eyes. And shadows, deceive. Can I see a figure: a person? a cross? a Christmas?

All three…

Eyes are such poor tools for sightings, on Christmas Eve.

*— December 2000*

## The Roughly Zones in May are upon us

Hear now the news: There are Roughly Zones in May.

Weather experts do not recognize "Roughly Zones" but such turbulence exists. Like wandering storms Roughly Zones pop up unexpected, ripping apart both hearts and the heartland, taking victims without regret.

It happened one ordinary day last week. I awoke to the fragrance of my front yard's peach tree blossoms. The morning breeze delivered the message, soft and sweet. It was a sun-rich morning, dappled by green tree shadows beyond the bedroom window's sash. The sash opened to a fresh day, a morning of spring. The wind spread my peach tree's blossom throughout the house. And, as my wife left for work, her hair perfume met the peach tree aroma, balancing, and finally merging.

I couldn't tell then, but hidden in the mixture, faint and fragrant, was the damage left behind by last night's storm. I thought this was just another safe spring morning in May. The trees so full, so thick and green. But then Crystal, the 8-year-old girl next door, came knocking. Crystal's habit (I encouraged her with cookies) is to bring my paper to me every morning. We say hello and Crystal, an avid reader of my paper before I see it, tells me the news.

These days I get almost all my news from Crystal. The worried look upon her young brow warned me of trouble. She stalled, chit-chatting some idle gossip,

"Hey Chuck, did you know a dog followed Kim right onto the school bus yesterday? I gave her my turkey sandwich. The dog I mean, not Kim. Dangerous things in schools these days, huh, Chuck?"

But then she let me have it right between the eyes,

"Sorry about your tree, Chuck. It was a good little tree."

Before leaving, my wife, dressed in a dark green suit, lifts her brown high heel shoes across the fallen peach tree. Damaged beyond repair. The tree I mean, not the wife. As Crystal said it really was a good little tree. From the porch screen door I see the tree, its green leaves still grasping life covered with dew. Even her blossoms still bloom. In fact, the tree had never looked lovelier than this morning, bent like a child in church kneeling to pray.

Gone so soon, so soon.

My wife looks up calling to me, but she's too far away. Maybe her lips say, "Sorry about your peach tree, dear." Me too. I am sorry for the news.

But here now the news:

"The dearest peach tree split last night in the wind. It wasn't such a windy night, not as windy as some, but windy enough to split wood. Investigators on the scene had no explanations, no suspects, and no clues. Human error is believed the cause. But beware the Roughly Zones. Film at eleven."

And I am home today, caring for the dead. A parade of children's funerals from Littleton, Colorado, breaks across my TV picture tube in living color. I leave the set muted, as a sort of silent respect for the dead. Compared to the Colorado tragedies my Peachtree is not really news. But I report it here anyway. More than report, I offer this exclusive scoop.

I fully confess to the crime.

This was indeed human error and not an act of God. I am the guilty one. But I did not act alone.

I blame and name poet Robert Frost as my co-conspirator in this premeditated act. It was he who gave me the thought to grow a peach in these uncertain Kentucky weather zones. Frost wrote in "There Are Roughly Zones,"

*What comes over a man, is it soul or mind—*
*That to no limits and bounds he can stay confined?*
*You would say his ambition was to extend the reach*
*Clear to the Arctic of every living kind.*
*Why is his nature forever so hard to teach*
*That though there is no fixed line between wrong and right,*
*There are roughly zones whose laws must be obeyed?*
*There is nothing much we can do for the tree tonight,*
*But we can't help feeling more than a little betrayed*
*That the northwest wind should rise to such a height*
*Just when the cold went down so many below.*

I alone planted the peach. And with the planting I alone sowed destruction's seed. The tree grew a few years, perhaps more by luck than by acclimation. It was like a child, really. It grew where it was planted and was a pleasure to watch it changing in the passing seasons. Then came this Roughly Zone, and snap.

And so, I am home to care for the broken tree. Sitting inside my safe home, I can smell the blossoms, still. They linger here among my practical breakfast of bacon, toast, and eggs. This meal is fresh cooked, but sits cold. Perhaps the light trace of hairspray distracts me?

After discarding the breakfast food, I will chainsaw the peach tree into firewood. Little tiny sticks that shall burn like candles in the fireplace tonight. And with the evening my wife returns, her hair smelling more like peach memory than of living blossoms. We will sit together by the fireplace watching the fresh green wood burn. The fire will give off a bit of heat but precious little light as we read the evening newspaper. She'll read the front page and do the crossword puzzle. I'll read the sports. And the peach tree embers will burn low, their soft green wood crying the news. *— May 1999*

# Migraines for Lent

I saw a white bird, what I thought was a dove, flying from a tree limb skyward. I noticed it out my truck's window as I drove from work, home. Home in mid-afternoon, home with a headache that had been pounding me for days.

It happened to be Ash Wednesday, and looking at the dove, I thought how like a cross he flew. Lifting and rising, rising above the tree line in three strong, rhythmic strokes. Climbing on this last day of February, February 28th, a crisscrossing into a clear sky.

Fearing a wreck I glanced at my rearview mirror and saw the road deserted save me, my white-speckled beard and face shining in the mirror of my old Ford truck. I had ashes on my forehead, black streaks like a crow. About then I discovered the bird outside my truck window was actually a crow.

It startled me discovering this, watching as it cleared the tree line, the white shimmering feathers darkening to a coal dust. Yes, a blackbird. Only just for that moment, there below the tree line, the sun had caught the bird, held it, so for an instant it appeared white.

But a blackbird sure enough.

My poor, pounding head labeled it a dove. I squinted and wondered how a blackbird could appear so white? And I prayed we had some aspirin, or Excedrin (or a big wooden mallet) at home, as I drove on, my head pounding. Soon tiny white and black spots, which from experience I know means a migraine's coming, fluttered around my eyeballs as the bird shot off.

Leaving, the crow looked less like a cross and more like a big "M" for migraine in the sky. What causes migraines, anyhow? I guess it depends upon the angle of the light. Or the speed of the flight. Or a certain weakness of mind known for turning a white dove into a blackbird. I was wondering if the blackbird was some migraine messenger. And said out loud, "If this pounding in my head gets any worse, next thing you know I'll be talking to myself."

Only about a mile or so to get home. A mile or so until sucking down a few extra-strength Excedrin. My head hurt so bad I thought I was about to die. Then I recalled a childhood chant, "Ashes to ashes, dust to dust. If the living doesn't kill you, the dying must."

Ash Wednesday, the beginning of Lent. The beginning of a season of self-denial. "Remember you are dust and to dust you shall return" is what they say, crossing your forehead in black. And I recalled as a child thinking how the ashes from our coal furnace turned not black but a soft and flaky white. Didn't the priest ever mark anybody's head with white ash? White and soft as a baby's butt. Soft and white as an old man's beard.

And I wished I could give up migraines for Lent.

*— March 2001*

# The winds of change are blowing

It's windy this evening. A loud, gruff, rip-roaring wind. A kite-flying wind, a season-changing wind, a spring-is-here wind.

Signs of spring are clear. The days get longer. The ground heaves with wet, thick, earthy smells. Backyard gardens sprout rakes and hoes and deep boot-prints. Seed catalogs wait inside roadside mailboxes that shake and clatter in the breeze.

Schoolboys and schoolgirls wait outside for the bus. Their winter coats give way to vinyl windbreakers, that is, if mom can persuade them to wear any coat at all. No matter, that howling wind would tear the breaker off a child.

Soon the bicycles will re-appear, and then kites and baseballs. Soon mom will hang last year's spring outfits on the backyard clotheslines for air. Like flags of spring, these clothes flap and beat and shout the news...something new is happening...

Drugstores pull back the St. Patrick's Day propaganda and herd the chocolate Easter bunnies out. Churches grow swollen with the Easter vigil. People feel for the season's light coats and bright colors with caution upon the church steps. Is it time yet? Dare I wear this? Dare I welcome spring? Or will winter rush back and grab my family?

Formalwear stores bulge with prom and wedding gowns. A young couple stands at the newspaper office with engagement pictures in hand. "When will they be printed? Why don't you print color? Can you save us a copy for our parents?" Next to them a woman complains, "Our paper was blown away by the wind last night, I want another. Why don't you put a rock on the papers—that wind blows strong by my house, don't you know?"

Papers swirl near the lake. A boy walks to the water's edge armed with his kite and his dad. It is the boy's first kite. It is the dad's first son. The wind blows at their vinyl jackets as the boy holds his kite by the tail. Is it windy enough yet, dad? Will it fly? Over the lake two kites already fly as another father watches his two brave daughters let out their string. An old fisherman smiles at the children flying kites but worries of tangling lines.

College kids take their spring break. One girl drives non-stop to the Texas gulf shore. She calls home announcing she made it, safe and sound. Pressing the phone to her ear mom hears the wind rattle in the county telephone lines. She imagines her daughter in Galveston dancing with Glen Campbell...Or is she imagining herself dancing?

Speaking from the beach into a red designer cell phone her already sunburnt daughter asks, "Who's Glen Campbell, Mom?" The 20-year-old college junior has to cover one ear to keep out the Gulf Stream's roar. "Mom I've met a boy from Tennessee, he played basketball this year, his name is Rudy. Have you heard of him Dad? Got to go now Mom. Sand's blowing in my cell phone. Love you mom, love you dad..."

Back in town by the old courthouse a homeless man unbuttons the top of his frayed, red flannel shirt. He sits on a worn bench seat. He is watching the wind blow sawdust up from the sidewalk where a pear tree has been cut. He wonders why the tree was killed before it had a chance to bloom in spring? Just like folks these days, killing a living thing before the bloom.

Near the courthouse the cars are parked along the sidewalk. Some have their windows rolled down. And the wind rushes, grabbing a sliver of pear tree carrying it inside the car across the dashboard. The old man laughs. It's been four months since he's seen the wind blow through a car.

This particular car is a new one; its owner comes out of a store carrying a fresh can of car wax. He looks 17 years old. The man pulls at his shirt and says, "This here flannel is older than you, boy." But the young man doesn't pay any attention as he starts his car. And the wind howls and blows. And the old man re-buttons his shirt, crosses his legs, and looks the other way. *— March 2001*

## Easter memories spring forth

My three earliest childhood memories of Easter morning are like three postcard images: a beach, a barn, and an umbrella.

The first picture postcard is a pink sunrise over a sandy beach. Our whole parish traveled to the Atlantic Ocean for Easter's dawn. I'd never been to the ocean before that Easter. Seeing the sunrise over the water led me to believe all beaches had huge wooden crosses hammered into the sand. Using the dumb logic a kid has, I believed Christ's cross (if you could get up close enough to it in church) would smell of creosote and the salty sea air.

The second postcard, the barn, was a place we always passed during the ride to church. This Easter morning my parents yelled, "Quick, Charles look at the barn's window!" Apparently a small horse, days old, stood there peering out. "That's a newborn," my folks said. I'd been asleep and hadn't seen the tiny horse at all. So what I remember is wondering how an old barn, its boards rattling in the spring wind, could be called "knew born."

The umbrella in my third Easter memory is on a sidewalk. After an Easter Sunday Mass I was following my parents as we headed for the parking lot and our sky-blue Buick. A young girl, maybe sixteen, was walking ahead on wobbly white, high heel shoes. It had been raining, almost snowing, on this cold Easter Sunday. The rain had stopped and the girl began balancing her steps using the umbrella, placing the point onto the sidewalk. Suddenly the tip stuck in a crack, standing the umbrella upright in the middle of the sidewalk.

My family stopped, stunned, afraid to touch the umbrella. My father whistled a low "Jesus H. Christ?" And I looked up ahead for the girl, knowing for certain she would turn around at any moment to retrieve her missing property. But she did not. My dad said, "I guess that's not a cross she wants to bear." Then mom smacked my dad with her purse for being sacrilegious. We circled the umbrella like you'd walk around a cold snake coiled to strike.

A beach, a barn, and an umbrella—not quite the holiest of Easter memories I'll grant you. But they stick in my mind and like self-addressed postcards they occasionally return to me. Recently in Glendale the creosote smell of train tracks put me back in front of that empty cross by the sea.

And after a rainstorm while walking the ECC campus my umbrella pointer got caught in the sidewalk. As I stared at that snake I quickly looked in front for a student wearing white high heels but there was none. (I guess the last time ANY student wore white high heels on campus Christ was still a carpenter's son.)

I found another "knew born" barn by chance. Just as the sunlight filled a window of a barn near the cove, I happened to look up. In the light I thought I saw a newborn foal's tiny head. I didn't. It wasn't. But now every time I pass that old barn I look and hope. What I hope to see is a young foal, blinking her eyes up towards a blue Easter sky. *—April 2000*

## Summer moments are fleeting favorites

Sometimes the entire summer becomes one moment.

That magical moment when the rising Kentucky heat, the ice cream truck's jingle, and the smell of freshly cut lawns all converge making the summer stand still. It is the moment when this summer becomes timeless and joins last summer and the summer before that. Until all the summers of your life stretch like telephone poles bound by cables of communication bearing lines of memory back from all the summers you ever knew and can never forget.

You know the moment. Sometimes it happens when the train whistle from Glendale sounds in the early light, just as you bend (oh, my bad back) down for the morning paper. The paper is still wrapped in its clear plastic shell. Unraveling the foil you feel the morning's dew and wish it would rain. Rain a good one because this dew won't grow those tomatoes.

But didn't you reach for that same paper last summer? Didn't you say the same rain prayer back then? Isn't this déjà vu all over again?

You know déjà vu, the repeating of a scene, a summer's sound, like a recurring message on your phone machine. It's when that plump girl in pink cotton shorts with Lima bean-shaped grass stains covering her bum is feeding the ducks. And with her Momma nowhere in sight, the girl falls face forward into the lake, not drowning, just soaking herself and scaring her Momma silly. Momma comes running to the rescue, her jewelry (silver bracelets, I think) jingling as she bends scooping pink britches from the water's edge. And how afterwards, after mom has carried pink britches safely back to their car, how the half-empty cellophane bag of wafers is left floating in the lake.

And every summer I'm watching the floating bread bag, wondering if this has all happened before? Waiting as, yes, right on cue, the bag dips from a nibbling hungry fish or two. The bread of life is bobbing slowly in the water like a flashing light. A memory buoy is unseen but always present, a déjà vu, coming with a flash of past memory, a ripple and a ring, something bobbing in the water, a flashing light in the night.

Who knows when your magical moment will hit? When it happens, perhaps you're cranking the handle on grandpa's ice cream machine. The same walnut wood handle your Grandpa turned for 83 years, bless his soul. If he were still alive, he'd say, "Son, summer's heat is the price we sinners pay for the pleasure of this homemade ice cream." And then he'd smile and say it's time and call for the spoons and bowls, the bowls and the spoons of ice cream.

And today clinking your spoon in a cold empty bowl, calling for seconds, are you certain you're not your grandfather just then? Holding his spoon, ringing his round bowl for more?

Such are the captured moments in time. You know them as well as I do. Maybe for you it comes from a song played on the radio. Maybe your song is like the song I hear coming from the utility truck parked across the street. A man in thick boots and a yellow hard hat is climbing the telephone pole. I recognize the song as an old Fab Four tune. A gasoline lawn mower engine from somewhere covers the tune and makes it hard to hear. But the lawn mower sputters and dies. In the empty seconds it takes for the mower to re-load, the Beatles sing out,

*"Closer, Doo-da-doo. Let me whisper in your ear...Doo-da-doo. Say the words you long to hearrrr."*

Then the lawn mower ripples back into life, drowning the Beatles away. But somewhere the song is always playing. Somewhere the man still climbs. The summer is always hot and humid, still and forever.

Forever too is my summer's memory of what a priest said about the utility poles. The sight of the man's yellow hard hat and his climbing has only just reminded me. From his tool belt I see black wire cutters sway like a clock's pendulum. I see the sun reflecting off his yellow plastic helmet. I see the heavy shears cut into the power line. That priest, years of Sundays ago, was also dressed in yellow. And his sermon cut like shears into the time-less-ness of summers.

The priest said every telephone pole was like a cross, and every cross was like a soul. And just as all the telephone poles were connected by cables, so too were all the souls on earth bound together. And we could pray to anyone at anytime just the same way we dialed the phone. Everyone and everything was connected. Just like Ma Bell's telephone line.

And this summer day while writing, someone keeps calling. I can hear the phone bell ring. Ringing like the bell of a spoon on a empty bowl of ice cream. Bells like round silver bracelets ringing. Ringing the same song I hear during that moment when every summer stands still. It's the song from the Power Company's truck. The song is beneath every summer's train whistle, and just above every ice cream trucks jingle. It's the song the priest meant to sing. It is the song that asks,

*"Listen, do you want to know a secret? Do you promise not to tell?"* —*June 1999*

# After 83 cards arrive

This year the Mrs. and I mailed out 83 Christmas cards. I am hoping for 83 cards in return. I know this is a selfish thought, expecting cards in reply...but I am crazy about Christmas cards. I love sending (and receiving) them.

Every year I save all the cards. I arrange them in categories: most poignant, best sacred message, best secular message, and best geometric design. I especially treasure the most creative home-made cards, and the funniest, the most lewd, most surprising. And so on.

I'd have to say Christmas cards are just about my favorite hobby of the season. So if anyone wants to send me a card, please do. In my silly game of Christmas card collecting, only cards with a stamp (not a metered machine mark) and delivered by a mailman count. Not Federal Express. Not UPS. If it gets slipped under the door at work or left on your desk, no dice. All cards have to come through the genuine flying eagles of the United States Post Office.

I said a minute ago I am expecting 83 cards back. One year (as a joke) I made up a form letter that looked like a bill collector's note warning the recipient of their overdo obligation. It read,

*"Dear Mr and Mrs. Procrastinator:*

*First Notice: You are past due responding to the Christmas card sent to you by Mr. Charles Spataro. There will be no further warnings. Your failure to comply will result in turning your account over to the North Pole collection agency. If you have already fulfilled this obligation, please disregard this notice and have a Merry Christmas."*

Great cards often come from the most unlikely places. My favorite card of all time came from my brother. Now you'd have to know my brother to appreciate his sending a card at all. Anthony hasn't sent a letter through the mail since we both wrote home from Camp Woeaweenick back in 1961. All he could think to say was to ask mom if she'd seen Roger Maris hit his 61st home run.

As I said, nothing very personal comes out of my brother Tony. He doesn't have a sentimental bone (how could we be brothers?) in his body.

But somehow he mailed the perfect card.

Anthony reached deep inside my psyche and pulled out my secret Christmas wish and served it up to me on a card like plum pudding. What I have always wanted to do was to take our Christmas tree, bulbs, lights, gifts,...the whole shooting match...tie it all to my boat and drift out into Harmony Cove. And just float out there all Christmas Eve under the stars. I'd take along a thermos of hot chocolate and a jug of eggnog. I'd keep Christmas cookies wrapped warm in Reynolds Wrap on my lap. I'd let the boat drift, past the glowing Christmas displays lining the shore. I'd be looking into every brightly-lit house, searching for a Christmas tree all-aglow. And I'd try to judge which family opened gifts on Christmas Eve, and who waited for morning's delight. Then, just as it began to snow, I'd wave to the brave souls all bundled up heading out to Midnight Mass.

As my brother's card shows, the stars on my tree would blend with the snow dotting the blackened night sky. The water surrounding my bobbing boat would reflect this sky until you couldn't be sure if the boat with its tree-lights blinking wasn't part of the floating cosmos.

And floating like a dream, sipping "spiked" eggnog I'd count echoes from the shore. I'll pass the time humming back Christmas songs, church hymns, and childlike laughter to the rows of houses. Maybe some kids would rush to their windows, point at the boat with its Blue Spruce rising eight-foot tall like a holiday lighthouse in the black night. And they'd call to their parents asking, "Mommy, is that Santa's boat? Does Santa deliver presents by boat? Daddy, does Santa's flying sleigh really, Float?"

And so, this Christmas Eve, after all 83 cards all arrive, I just may try fitting my tree into the boat. I've got my brother's card for inspiration: but I'm kind of worried how far the tree's electric extension cord will stretch… *— December 2000*

# New Year's Day 1999—a chance to mind travel

I'm sitting at the porch's sliding glass door, a thin layer of Plexiglas and my bathrobe is all that is separating me from the bitter cold outside on this new year's morning.

Behind me my wife is talking, puttering around the kitchen, feeding the cats, rattling the breakfast dishes, and doing a million things to engage me in conversation…

But I'm out there by the lake testing the ice and cold.

I vaguely hear her ask if I think we'll bundle up and try driving to town. I hear her wondering if the car will start and if the icy roads are worth risking the journey…

I am on the roads already…

Out beyond our property are the cove and the lake beyond. A small island lies frozen in the cove, connected to shore by a rickety, old wooden bridge. The bridge shakes in the wind as my wife adjusts the radio from a local country station to National Public Radio. I tug tight on my bathrobe and I hear a whistle as my wife rushes to shut the burner beneath the kettle. NPR reports Ft. Knox is holding steady at 10 degrees above zero. The bridge doesn't look steady; it trembles in a wind chill surely colder than 10 degrees…

My wife says she needs to call her mother, to see if they are okay in this cold. Outside the wind's whistle blends with our tea kettle's whine…

I can hear my wife asking her mother about the roads. My father-in-law will have been out, driving to McDonalds for coffee and a biscuit like he always does—rain, sleet, snow, or shine. He is retired but drives a school bus. A more careful, road-conscious driver never guided a Hardin County yellow bus. Subtract 55 years and this same prudent driver was racing stock cars on dirt tracks from here to Campbellsville and back. Throwing the same caution, which today he holds so dearly, to the youthful wind…

Behind me I can hear their conversation turn to New Year's Eve. My wife is trying to describe how I re-decorated the Christmas tree into a New Year's tree. I placed party hats and horns in amongst the Christmas bulbs and hung a black plastic New Year's Eve hat upon the Angel on the tree's top. The hat looks like something "Frosty the Snowman" might wear, but it says "Happy New Year 1999" in rainbow colors…

A dusting of white snow covers the lake. Brief gusts swirl the snow and in the harsh January sunshine rainbow colors dance snow-man-like jigs across the lake. I notice how similar these colors are to the Happy New Year letters on the black hat atop our evergreen Christmas tree.

Last year some lake people tossed their discarded Christmas tree onto the frozen lake.

Vandalism?

Perhaps. It was exactly one year ago I sat here watching the wind ripple across these castaway trees catching bits of tinsel and forgotten paper angels as it passed.

I walked on the thin ice (my usual style in all things) retrieving these dead trees. Dragging them deep into the surrounding woods to a place of timelessness. A place I bring all my Christmas trees on New Year's Day. A clearing deep inside the woods which now holds Christmas trees forming a teepee-shaped pile, a haven for birds and wild life during the cold winters' freeze.

I am at this spot now, as my wife brings me a plate of scrambled eggs and toast. She tucks a napkin inside my bathrobe and asks me to put down my pen and paper and eat…

I am at the Christmas tree teepee watching stray bits of tinsel quiver in the cold. I count the trees back to the first Christmas, the first New Years we spent at the lake.

"You know, Chuck," says my neighbor when we happen to come upon the teepee in summer, "maybe you should have left them trees where you found them. Maybe folks dumped their trees on the lake for a reason."

"What reason?"

"Well, I hear catfish like to make their nests in trees and such near the shore. Maybe they left them trees there to attract catfish eggs, you reckon?"

I am under the ice now. Swimming around layers upon layers of catfish Christmas trees. It is a new year and I wonder what will come? I can hear my wife above me through the muffling ice. She is cooking catfish for lunch. She is talking to her mother on the phone asking if the roads are plowed, salted, and clear.
*— January 1999*

# September's flagpole clang

When I hear the flagpole ring in September, the first month of fall, I think how another year is passing. I can hear the metal clasp clanging against the tall, silver pole whenever the wind blows. It rings in an irregular clang, a metallic *ping-pong, gong,* (pause, pause,) *ping-pong gong*, almost asking, "So soon? Has summer gone so soon?"

The September wind has arrived at Harmony Cove. It's still summer to be sure, but with the ninth month comes a hint of autumn. Breezes brush and bounce the flagpole's cord more often now than during the summer's night. And the flagpole by the lake keeps watch, ringing like a sentry's bell. There's a brush, and then a rustle-ringing in of fall. Depending upon the wind's direction and the amount of competition from basketballs bouncing in driveways, I can hear October coming soon, just miles away like a train whistle blowing.

*Ping-pong, gong. Ping-pong, gone* is the plentiful waste of summer's time. The flagpole's lonely song is the sound I listen for at first light while making coffee. It is the sound I hear locking the doors and closing the windows at final light before bed. For me, the pole's chime is a living, breathing friend, a heartbeat from the lake, beating as it crosses off the days from May to December.

During the young summer months, teenage lifeguards tend the pole. They come to the water's edge sleepy-eyed, yawning from late night drive-in movie dates at Fort Knox. Their tanned, bare feet carry them and the American flag from the pool house to the pole, starting the day. With towels wrapped around their tank suits they appear exotically draped in sarongs, worshiping youth and the summer's time.

And after a sun-filled day telling kids, "Walk, DON'T RUN!" these all-American girls leave their life stands and lower the flag, folding it between them, storing it for tomorrow. Some weekends (more than I'd be willing to say) the sight of a sarong-legged teenager carefully, almost tenderly, lowering Old Glory so its sacred colors don't touch the ground, has brought a tear to my eye.

A tear shed for the passing summer days, going, going, gone.

And when Labor Day passes and the pool closes, as it must, no lifeguards remain to tend the flagpole. Only the *ping-pong, gong* (pause, pause) *ping-pong, gone* remains.

It's funny how this sound can become a flag's red, white, and blue. Funny too, how in winter's coldest grip, the echoing flagpole brings back summer's pleasant sensations like the scent of suntan lotion mixed with chlorine. Or the sound of children begging their mothers for a quarter for another dripping rainbow snow cone.

Drippings gone, all *ping-pong gong.*

Today an old Sinatra tune croons from across the lake. It tells how the days dwindle down to a precious few, September, November. Hearing the deceased singer's voice call from somewhere beyond the cove is, curious. Was it Ol' Blue Eyes, or just some big Blue Heron echoing for its mate?

Do today's teenagers play Sinatra? Surely not. This tune must come from some old fisherman's boat. A bass buddy fallen asleep with his transistor radio tuned to WHAS for the weather report, perhaps. But now the report is an old Sinatra signature song slipping out, about the time slipping from May to December.

Waiting for this Sinatra song to end somehow isn't quite so lonely with the flagpole's gentle accompaniment ringing. There, in the background is the clang of my steady sentry. The comforting *ping-pong* and *gong* from an old friend. As fall's soft winds carry the familiar ping-pong and gong, I think of sarongs and summer nights and their plentiful waste of time, their plentiful waste somehow, so endurable. *—September 1999*

# Fruitcake: unstoppable, improbable, unpalatable

I believe there is one great truth holding our universe together. Einstein tried desperately to discover this "universal theory" but went to his grave in ignorance. $E=MC^2$ was close, but the formula that truly binds us all together is: Christmas fruitcake can be created, but it can neither be eaten nor destroyed.

How true? To test out this theory let's conduct an experiment. Go to your kitchen. Open up the refrigerator door and look all the way back on the bottom-most shelf. Look deep, deep beyond the Thanksgiving leftovers. Beyond the cottage cheese box now bubbling out a green ooze. Look deep past the Fourth of July deviled eggs made by Aunt Mabel, eggs that now resemble black eyes wrapped in plastic. Look deep and boldly, going where no man has gone before, to the very depths of the bottom left corner in your refrigerator. There, covered under a thin layer of prehistoric ice, is last Christmas' fruitcake from your grandmother.

Proof positive: Fruitcakes can be neither eaten nor destroyed.

This sad fact has global implications. Our tiny and fragile planet Earth is becoming contaminated with the tonnage of generations of fruitcake bakings. I believe it was Carl Sagan who said a virtual fruitcake-fratricide is taking place on spaceship Earth. Sagan believes billions and billions of indestructible fruitcakes will soon outnumber the human population of our planet.

Scientists around the world have been struggling to discover a means of fruitcake disposal. You may be familiar with some of the failures to date. A team of scientists recently attempted to bury the fruitcakes. For a period of seven years the cakes were stored successfully on the West Coast.

But then the disaster the media called Mount St. Helens occurred.

One New York scientist, Dr. Georgia E. Claxton, believed she could submerge the cakes underwater. As any Love Canal area resident can tell you, however, this project met with only moderate success.

The ancient people of Egypt never mastered a technique of destroying their fruitcakes, but they did employ a clever use for the material. What use? The Egyptian word for pyramid comes from the Greek word "Frymcyke," meaning "built of fruitcakes."

China, being a nation of millions of people, has seen its share of fruitcakes. The ingenious and even more inscrutable

Chinese hid their fruitcake secret for centuries until President Richard Nixon stumbled upon the truth.

During Nixon's acclaimed visit to China's mainland, he was given a tour of the Great Wall. Nixon reportedly said, "This is a magnificent structure, but (sniff, sniff) isn't that fruitcake I smell?"

The only storage-disposal research in the United States that has had any success has come in the top-secret atomic energy lab down in Oak Ridge, Tenn. It seems all fruitcakes shipped to and received by U.S. servicemen since 1953 have been routed to Oak Ridge for experimental study.

No one knows for certain what has become of the Oak Ridge fruitcakes. Some people suspect they formed a country-western singing group…

Presently, there is only one method for disposing of fruitcakes that is approved by the U.S. Surgeon General. According to his latest "Fruitcake Report," the following steps are advised: 1) Open your box of fruitcake immediately. 2) Cut off one slice (an often impossible and sometimes fatal task). 3) Repackage your fruitcake and store deep within your icebox until next Christmas. When Christmas approaches you are advised to mail the package to someone else, preferably someone with an iron stomach or a deep, deep refrigerator. *— December 1984*

# The night before the night before Christmas

Dear Santa:

Elizabethtown is a quiet town on the night before the night before Christmas. It's cold here in Kentucky, so cold that the deer out by Freeman Lake have to paw the water's edge to crack through the ice. And the stained glass windows on St. James Church glisten with extra colors painted on by Jack Frost.

We are waiting for you to come.

Out down Glendale way the gift shops and the Whistle Stop Restaurant still tingle with the scent of spiced tea. These stores are closed now. The shoppers and eaters are home asleep. Main Street in Glendale is asleep. Fireplace smoke mixes with the snow white clouds beneath a Christmas moon.

All is in waiting for you to come.

Radcliff has an all-night doughnut shop open and bright. The counter girl is leaning on her cash register. She is a student at the college. She just finished with final exams. She is wondering which is worse: taking finals or agreeing to work tonight and the night before Christmas. She is waiting for her shift to end at midnight. The soldier at the end of the counter wants to catch her eye for more coffee, black.

They are waiting for you to come.

Over in Hardin Memorial Hospital a nurse is smoking a cigarette while looking out the third floor window. It is almost midnight. She wishes she could be home in bed. The boy in Room 309 (just a boy, 19 at most) has finally fallen asleep. The police think he must have fallen asleep at the wheel. No ID. She can see the Christmas tree in the movie theater across the highway. The red tip of her cigarette burns like the red lights on that distant tree.

A police officer patrols the shops at Governor's Manor. He pauses at the Deli and thinks of the rich New York Cheesecake inside. What he wouldn't give for a hot cup of coffee and a piece of Joe's cheesecake right now. He tests the door. Locked. Safe. He turns facing the highway and shivers in the cold night air. There's a red light flickering from a hospital window. Must be a light from a Christmas tree. Those nurses do a good job of making the hospital feel the holiday spirit.

In the hospital they are waiting also.

The local DJ welcomes his listeners to the night before the night before Christmas show—all Christmas music, all night long. That was Frank Sinatra singing, "Have Yourself a Merry Little Christmas." Now this is the late, great Nat King Cole with a tune written by Mel Torme'…"The Christmas Song,"…so sit back and maybe toss a few chestnuts on the fire, you're listening to Hardin County's best radio station W…

At the community college a radio plays in a deserted lecture hall. The night janitor is wiping down the smoky blackboards. His portable radio plays the velvet-smooth voice of Nat King Cole. The janitor strokes the board clean to the music's beat. Blackboards. Black-voice. Tiny tots with their eyes aglow will find it hard to sleep, tonight.

"*They know that Santa's on his way. He's loaded lots of toys and goodies on his sleigh. And every mother's child is gonna try—to see if reindeer really, know how to fly…*"

With almost a silent crack a deer's hoof pushes through the ice at Freeman Lake. It lifts its head as if to see if the tiny pop attracted an enemy. Sensing none, it lowers down (as in human prayer) to drink. Across the lake a second deer punches through the ice. At the crack they stare each other still. Brown eyes glow yellow-cold in the moonlight. And blink. Friend. Fellow wader. Friend.

*"Though it's been said many times, many ways, Merry Christmas. Merry Christmas. Merry Christmas to you."*

*— December 1984*

# Goodbye, Bluegrass!

On this first day of April I submit for your kind consideration my final column. Effective today, I'm accepting a position with the Philadelphia Bulletin as a Lifestyle Editor.

Saying farewell to this paper and to this community is a difficult assignment. Right now I can only think of Joni Mitchell's sad and sweet song, "*Don't it always seem to go, that you don't know what you've got till it's gone…*"

Let me say this April first goodbye by remembering what Kentucky's "got" and by adding how much I'll miss it when I'm gone.

I'll miss the casual beauty of the horse land. Casual I say only because it is so widespread. Turn off almost any country road and you'll see it. The single, old broken-down barn. The pair of horses, one old, one young, their noses gently nudging the bluegrass.

Suddenly the younger horse sprints away. To where and for what reason? Who knows, there is no answer. But in its irascible dance is the promise of youth, while in the older horse's steadfastness lies the wisdom of maturity.

I love being close to horses. I'll miss them. I'll miss seeing the wet bags of breath they can leave hanging on a winter's morn. Breath like smoke from a pent-up locomotive's engine, except this engine runs not on coal but on heart and oats.

And I'll miss the secret fishing holes I've discovered these past five years. Many's the time I've pulled more than my fair share out of Freeman Lake. And many's the time I've gone there just for the lake's beauty.

I've sat and watched a silent mist rise from the Freeman water near dawn. There, the very silence says, "Kentucky." And as I snapped my fishing line into the lake, I've heard the water swallow as if to say, "Oh." Putting these two sounds together, I was hearing "Oh Kentucky" long before Gov. Brown and his wife, Phyllis, did.

Maybe most of all I'll miss talking to the school kids in Hardin County. I loved to visit their classrooms and join in to recite the Pledge of Allegiance.

I'll never forget the time after one pledging when we talked about what it means. One boy asked me who was Richard.

"Huh?" I replied. "What Richard?"

"You know," the kid said. "We pledge allegiance to the flag of the United States of America. And to the Republic for Richard Stands…"

It's curious, but another thing I'll miss is the church steeple that towers over Elizabethtown. This tall soldier of faith is like a dear friend. It symbolizes the strength of vigilance of the Kentuckians I've come to know.

My hope is that this sentry will welcome me back should I ever return. (You can never tell.) Maybe, just maybe, the steeple's part lighthouse—guiding the way for both departures and returns of April Fools.

*(Editor's Note: Readers are forewarned that the Philadelphia Bulletin folded more than a year ago...and it is April Fool's Day.) —April 1983*

# Society's trick on Emma May

After 72 years, arthritis settled in the fingers of Mrs. Emma May like ice. Emma didn't like looking at her hands. They used to be so lovely. Her husband Ned called them princess hands when they first met. Ned died last February.

Since his death, Emma used her hands less. Without a husband there was less cooking to do and less sewing. "Even less reason to fix the bed every morning," Emma thought.

It was funny how her hands ached more now that she called upon them so much less. But pain or no pain—today she would use those crooked claws. Today she needed to be up early to fix the bed and get straight to work. Today was Halloween.

Every year Emma made homemade fudge. Brown fudge, white fudge—fudge so thick, yet so creamy, kids came from outside the county to trick or treat the May house.

Fixing her bed, Emma enjoyed the excitement of planning a busy day in her kitchen. Halloween would be nice. The kitchen would be warm again. The house would have voices and children again. Halloween came just in time...

Emma walked through the living room past the cold fireplace. Halloween cards from her children, some from Atlanta and some from Vermont, lined the mantle. "Send your hungry grandchildren your love and your fudge," they said.

Brown fudge, white fudge—fudge so rich it made Halloween a May Family Holiday as special as Christmas. Emma nodded to the cards. "I'll bake you all an extra batch!"

Pumpkin, a large and lazy tabby cat, also found Halloween special. Pumpkin became dizzy with delight at the smell of homemade fudge. It made him spin round and round as if there were catnip in the air. During the slow cooking of the fudge, Pumpkin stalked the kitchen floor. Should Emma's stiff hands let a slice of the rich chew fall—it was as good as gone.

Oddly enough, in all her years of making fudge, Emma never noticed Pumpkin's sweet tooth.

As Emma began pulling out the fudge pans, a moody Pumpkin wondered how he would survive Halloween night without the generous Mr. May…

The work went well. Emma's fingers ached but she made slow, steady progress. Over the years she'd developed a practiced efficiency in fudging.

As the day passed, the October leaves crackled against the kitchen sink window. More than once Emma reached for the bottle of extra-strength pain relief capsules. She'd just bought them. They were what Ned had always made her take for pain. But, each time she put the bottle back on the kitchen windowsill.

"I don't know why I keep buying those darn pills! Without Ned around to open the bottle cap, I'll never be able to use them!"

Emma cried. The pain in her hands and the memory of Ned hurt as one. She bent over the sink for a moment as Pumpkin came closer and rubbed the old woman's leg.

Emma dried her tears on a dishtowel and ran some hot tap water over her sore fingers. That helped a little. By five o'clock there were four large pans of fudge, cooled, cut and almost ready.

She judged there would be enough for 50 children. Finally, a sturdy piece of waxed paper and a newspaper rubber band sealed each treat airtight.

By 7 p.m. all was ready. Only when the doorbell rang did Emma realize she hadn't changed out of her nightgown. No matter. She knew the kids would figure she'd just gotten ready for bed.

At the door was the Miller boy and his babysitter. They were from the next block but they always made the May house their first stop.

"Hello Eddie," said Emma without much noticing his pirate patch, makeup, and blackened teeth. "Help yourself to some fudge."

The boy paused. "Sorry Mrs. May, but I can't. The kids have all been told not to accept any candy that hasn't been pre-sealed by the store. It's Halloween, you know. People are funny."

Emma shut the door as the children and Pumpkin slipped out. She was shaking. Her day, her special day, was ruined. The ice in her fingers throbbed with pain. Emma turned for the kitchen, determined to open that bottle of pain relief pills.

*— October 1982*

# Ode to Father's Day

*Father's Day brings memories*
*As every father knows, so*
*Tell us Pops can you recall*
*When last you touched your toes?*

To the best of my knowledge, I'm not a father. Being thus "sans-sibling" allows an impartial viewpoint for me to comment on a few do's and do-not's in the celebration of Pops Day.

The No. 1 do-not involves buying gifts for the old man. Do not give Dad underwear or socks for Father's Day—even if it's what he needs. Dads may not be very bright but they are rarely stupid, either. Any gift that says "Fruit of the Loom" instead of "I Love You" is a letdown.

Of course being a dad, he'll accept his underwear like a man. He may mumble some polite thank you. But even blockheads like fathers can sense a certain negative vibration from so uncourtly a gift as boxer shorts.

Notice any subliminal messages in dad's acceptance?

Having been warned not to buy underwear, you might wonder, "What else is there?" Plenty. Just think a minute. What is it most fathers want but seldom get in their married life? To be the boss.

Making a dad the boss is no easy matter. Usually Mom already has dibs on that title. But you can at least make the old bird "feel" like the boss by pretending to obey a few of his orders on Father's Day. Let him rule the roost. Maybe even let him choose the channel to watch on TV. I tell you such sudden power will make his head swim.

*Happy Happy Father's Day*
*And you deserve the best.*
*Today we'll treat you like the boss,*
*And give poor Mom some rest.*

Teenagers especially need tips on how to honor their fathers on his day of days. Do not try to turn your "square old dad" into a "hip cat" overnight. He may love you very much, but he might not be able to relate to an extra-large-sized Pac ManT-shirt. He'll probably think his new E.T. shirt means something dirty in Latin. And, if you give him a shirt he can understand, like a Dallas Cowboys Cheerleaders design, then Mom will be on your case.

Another warning for teens: don't even consider buying him an album. To your dad, the "Motels" are still buildings like Travel Lodge and Days Inn. Chances are your father thinks "ABBA" is something he remembers Fred Flintstone telling Barney to do.

And teens, think how embarrassed you'll be if Dad thanks you for his new Willie Nelson record by saying he didn't know Ozzie and Harriet had two sons in the music industry.

*Two bits, four bits,*
*Six bits a dollar.*
*Our dad's the greatest*
*Even with his ring around the collar!*

Here's a "do" for Dad's Day. Take dear ol' Dad to the movies. However, sibling discretion is advised. Better pick out a nice, safe "G-rated" Disney film. If you introduce Dad to all the violent and sexy "PG" and "R" flicks you've been seeing, it may be your last picture show. Then Brooke Shields will have to grow old without you watching.

Whatever movie you finally decide on, don't make the mistake of going to a drive-in. If Dad learns how little drive-ins have changed since he and Mom were dating, it will mean the end of your pilgrimages into the passion pit. Stick to Disney and indoor theater, and be sure to ask him to buy you some Milk Duds.

*Hidee Hey, Hidee Ho*
*Who's our big Daddio?*
*Oh my gee. Oh my gosh,*
*He's the one whose hair is lost!*

A Father's Day card is a must "do." Select one to describe him as he thinks he is. If Dad's a sports nut, get a card with Joe Namath on the cover. Is cooking Dad's game? Get the card shaped like a chef's cap. Remember, it is important not to remind Dad of who he really is. Fat and bald dads hate cards with pictures of Uncle Fester.

How you sign the card is vital. Again the key here is not to threaten. For example, never sign by saying, "Don't worry Dad, you'll find another job some day." Or, if you and Mom have split up from Dad, remember not to say, "And Mom's new boyfriend wishes you a Happy Father's Day, too…"

A homemade card with a simple thought is always a nice touch. Here's one I sent my dad:

*On Father's Day, On Father's Day*
*We honor the old codger.*
*On Father's Day, On Father's Day*
*We praise the once-artful dodger.*
*We'd like to say,*
*How good it's been*
*To live with you*
*As your hair grows thin.*
*On Father's Day, On Father's Day*
*We'd like to say we love you.*
*On Father's Day, On Father's Day*
*Accept this tie and ditty.*
*On Father's Day your special day*
*You make our hearts feel giddy.*
*We love you so, words can't express*
*Our simple need for your caress.*
*And so just rest in bed*
*Make Sunday last, 'cause*
*We've paid Mom to cut the grass*
*On Father's Day, On Father's Day.* —*June 1982*

# Walking to Derby

Back a good walk in the woods our Derby waits for spring. She is a pure white statue, three feet tall, a maiden poised pouring (water, milk, or memories?) onto a small patch of Lenten Roses. Frozen like the tin-man in mid-action, Derby waits in silence.

My wife and I bought our statue on Kentucky Derby Day, a day that most Kentuckians know as the first day of spring, when we plant our gardens without fear of frost. Derby's location is not quite precise. I sort of know where she is, but it's not a well-worn path. No perfect map marks the road to finding her. But the trail is familiar once I'm upon it. I look forward to seeing Derby, as one who is traveling on a familiar road welcomes landmarks not so much for guidance but for company.

As I walk seeking Derby, I reflect on how walking to Derby is a duty, a dance, and a ritual like winding a clock or cleaning a gun. A task done less for its pragmatic value as for its respect to life's balance and obedience to time's ballet. As I walk, it is this year and past years, rolled into one. I remember many such February walks from my childhood. Walks taken after Valentines Day with a favorite aunt, Aunt Margaret.

My Aunt Margaret had a statue of the Virgin Mary out deep in the woods. It was nearly a mile's walk to Mary. The statue was near a stream, but off to one side, in a nest of green ferns and Lenten Roses. The weekend after Valentines Day Auntie M (she hated when we called her that) always announced she was hiking to visit the Holy Mother and any child who was brave enough to go along had better dress warm.

So we walked. Aunt M didn't know a thing about the woods. And my brother and I walked with Auntie M just to catch her getting lost. I'm certain she always did, but never let on. When she'd get that "I'm lost in the woods look" my brother would turn to me and say, "Toto, I don't think we're in Kansas anymore." Which is when I'd start barking (I was such a kid) causing Auntie M to shake her finger at us both. Then she'd press boldly on in search of Mary.

And after thirty, forty, or fifty-five minutes of brisk hiking (depending on how lost she got?) we'd find her. Mary was tall, almost five feet. She wore a round spiked crown, and looked more like pictures I'd seen of Joan of Arc than of the Blessed Mother. She was beautiful, also fierce looking, not a teenager but a woman full of power and life. I always wondered how Aunt Margaret got her statue way out there in the first place?

And, I always wanted to have that statue. Not because I'm super religious or I believe in miracles. But if you knew my Aunt then you understood her finding this statue deep in the woods each February was a minor miracle. Allowing us kids to journey with her took a certain amount of faith upon my parent's part.

My Aunt Margaret has been dead for many years. And for many years I have had my "Derby" set out deep in the Harmony

Cove woods. After Valentine's Day I go out seeking her, getting lost as I go. I like to think Auntie M comes walking with me, laughing about Kansas as we go. Together we find a statue near the Lenten Roses. *— February 2001*

# Christmas presents are memories from past

*O holy night*
*O come let us adore him*
*O little town of Bethlehem*
*O Christmas tree*
*O come, all ye faithful*
*O star of wonder, star of night*
*O night divine*
*O you better not shout, you better not cry...*

Pieces of Christmas songs can run through your head in no apparent order. They just play like music in a dream. Such music can trigger memories of Christmases past.

As a boy's choir on TV sings "O Holy Night" we recall not one specific Christmas, but a calliope of past and present Christmases. These many images may blur together. We see "one" holiday in which everyone is young, is healthy, is happy.

The memory of a single year can be a blend of images also. A joining of impressions, true and imagined. A kind of newsreel Christmas carol...

A gray morning. A December morn. Snow is falling, filling an empty city street. It's cold. A soldier thinks it's very cold as he stands watch in front of a union hall. His breath makes smoke. The union hall's steps are icy and blocked by snow.

Snow has capped his helmet. Snow has filled his rifle barrel. He shifts his gun and a pound of snow drops to the ground. It is quiet. It is Poland.

An expectant mother touches her new roundness. She is pretty. She is young. A gown of creamy, pale silk wraps tight around her stomach. She curls her legs beneath herself like a child.

She has been reading a children's Christmas story, but she has been crying, too. Her legs do not curl about herself as well as before. Read, read the story and do not notice. Read softly to...herself?...read gently to...her baby? Read firmly now to the future King of England.

Christmas colors reflect the electric tree upon the White House walls. The President strolls in the garden. A Marine snaps to attention as he passes by. The president notices the guard's boots. Polished black.

The Christmas tree is also reflected in the blackness. The President looks at the young man's face and shivers a friendly smile. "Cold this morning, isn't it soldier?" The young man looks straight away...

Inside the White House he remembers. Lying on an emergency room table, he was cold. He lay looking at his own polished black shoe. The doctors' white gowns were reflected in the hospital neon light. "I sure hope you are all Republicans..."

A mother asks the man to bless her child. The baby cold in a December afternoon cries. Waa Hee, Waa Heee. The Pope smiles and touches it with a sign of the cross. Waa Hee. Waa Hee. Waa Heeeeeeeee...

That sound. The sound of a siren. He remembers. An Italian ambulance siren is rushing him away. Waa Hee. Waa Hee. Hur-Ry. Hur-Ry. Hur-Ry.

The Pope turns to the crowd and says, "Patri, Patri, Patri...Blessed be, blessed be, blessed be the children. The President looks out his window and prays. What a lovely tree, what a lovely tree. Down an alley the Polish soldier thinks he hears a young woman cry out: Save me, somebody save me and my baby.

In her bedroom, the young princess is almost asleep. She turns on her side and feels a pain from where the child lay. Hush now. You better not shout, you better not cry... *—December 1981*

# In terms of respect, he gets jack

With October just around the corner, the letters should be pouring in—letters addressed to Mr. John T. Frost. You might know him by his nickname Jack.

As the designated Hardin County Jack Frost mail drop, I can tell you business is slow. It's a pity, because Jack Frost works twice as hard as most elves and gets no respect.

We practically ignore the buckskinned gadabout. Another October is upon us and who do you think will get all our attention? Not Jack Frost, but his half-brother Jack-o-Lantern, that's who. It's just not fair.

The elf of color and crystal deserves better. Jack busts his buckskin to paint the color and icy crystal of fall. He single-handedly turns summer's tired green into autumn's vibrant red, yellow, and gold. Unassisted, he etches prism-like patterns on cold, sparkling windowpanes.

Jack's up early each morning dancing from wood to wood, and from window to window leaving behind his lacy, white breath and colorful footprints. And yet, he doesn't even have a holiday named after him.

In November he's still on the job, but some dumb turkey grabs the limelight. And we all know December belongs to the fat man with polar elves. If it wasn't for Nat King Cole's brief mention of "Jack Frost nipping at your nose," this valiant elf of frost would be a complete unknown.

For shame! It's time we gave Jack Frost his just deserves. Jack has earned a few fan letters from the people. Since tomorrow is October, "tis the season to be frosty," let's start sending in those cards and letters to Jack.

But please, I'm begging you—think before you write! Some of the letters I've been getting are just terrible. I'm ashamed to even show them to Jack. For example:

*Dear Jack Frost: You're no big deal. How come you don't deliver presents? I think you'd be more popular if you said, "Ho, ho, ho" and delivered presents. Leave coloring trees to Mother Nature.*

*Dear Jack: I know all about you. I wanted to write this letter to say you're my hero. I hope someday I can grow up to be as nimble and as quick and able to jump over a candlestick just like you.*

*Dear Jack: Our entire third grade thinks you're the greatest! But tell me, weren't you scared when you fought that giant after climbing the beanstalk?*

*Dear Jack: Thanks a lot! Last Saturday Mom took me to McDonald's for lunch. I got pie for dessert, so I stuck in my thumb and was about to say, "What a good boy am I!" when it burned me so bad I spilled my Coke. Thanks for nothing!*

*Dear Mr. Frost: I hate you. Last fall you killed my vegetable garden. Daddy says you hate farmers. I hope you trip over your elf shoes and your nose gets frostbitten.*

Honestly now! These kids don't even know who Jack Frost is! Just look at that last letter. Obviously the writer is referring to Jack's mean and ugly older brother, Heavy Frost.

Heavy Frost is a bad elf. He wears a black leather jacket and rips around the countryside on a motorcycle. It's Heavy Frost who kills vegetables and fruit. But somebody has to tell the children about Jack Frost so kids don't confuse him with Heavy.

Gosh, the two look nothing alike. Heavy Frost wears his hair long and has a grizzly rough beard. With his black jacket and beard, Heavy looks like a Hell's Angel riding an "ice chopper."

Clearly this is not Jack. Jack Frost is a sensitive artist, not some motorcycle monkey. Jack gently touches Mother Nature with his fine brushes and paint. Jack gradually dresses the seasons for change, like a painter or a poet.

But unless Jack Frost gets some more recognition, people are bound to go on confusing him with other elves. So listen people, spread the word: Jack Frost ain't Heavy, that's his brother.

Adults and children wishing to write Jack Frost may do so in care of: Letter to Jack
P.O. Box 430
Elizabethtown, KY 42701

— *September 1981*

# Labor Day's a time for change

So endeth another Labor Day. And so backeth we go.

Workers go back to jobs. TV viewers go back to daytime soaps and game shows while Jerry Lewis goes back to bed. And life has a rhythm and season for all things.

Summer toys drift up from the tall grassy bushland of backyard playgrounds to rest a season in the garage. Baseball mitts, some carefully oiled, some not, are tossed under beds and into backs of closets.

Footballs are revived to regulation size and weight. The tribal grunt of a kid smashing his 12-year-old head into a 10-year-old's helmet is heard round the neighborhood. Softball-playing fathers stay home on Sunday afternoons. They watch TV football.

Phyllis George Brown is back in the minds and hearts of these dads.

And the kids go back to school. Once bare, brown toes pinch inside unrelenting Buster Brown shoes. Once sun-bleached cowlicks are slickered down. And the battle moves from outside to inside—the boys vs. the girls.

Lucy Snartgrass was my enemy. She was the original Wonder Woman. Tall, tanned, and the most gifted athlete in seven blocks, Lucy ruled the summer games. She peppered poor Mrs. Luckman's old apple tree out in center field with her classic line drives.

If Lucy had even an average summer at the plate (say about .425, 44 homers, 99 apples knocked down), the Luckmans ate applesauce every night. One summer we lost two center fielders who crashed into the tree chasing a Lucy liner.

The Luckman's yard was without a warning track. But then again, most things connected with Lucy came without warning, like the day Lucy became Lucille.

It was the day after Labor Day. The gang lined up at the bus stop as usual. I got there late because my preschool sister (the rat) stuck white shoelaces on my new brown shoes. Making the correction caused me to miss the bus stop gossip.

It wasn't hard to tell what the gossip was about. Lucy was a woman.

In the brief time that passed from her last line drive off Mrs. Luckman's tree till today, Lucy aged 12 years. She'd gone from a crafty 13-year-old shortstop to a 25-year-old woman with eyelashes and lipstick. She announced that her name was now Lucille.

We believed her. She wore a preppy skirt that gave her real legs. We'd all seen her legs before, but that was in the summer cutoff jeans. Then she had legs like the rest of us, full of insect bites and scraped knees.

But these legs were different. They grew out of a pair of high-heeled sandals and reminded you of Miss Bussman, the new public librarian.

And Lucy, uhh, that is, Lucille, walked funny. She sort of swished in those sandals. She still boarded the bus in one long stretching stride...but somehow we never watched her do it like we did on that first day of school.

I soon realized what she was up to. Lucy had spent the entire summer beating the guys at baseball. Now she was getting ready to beat us at school. Classes hadn't even started yet and she had a two-legged lead. Here the rest of us were, still runny-nosed kids waiting to return to school, and Lucy was a co-ed, a woman obtaining an education.

On board the bus she got the first seat without a fight. She smiled and stretched out those bare legs till her bare, sandaled toes hung lazily into the aisle. Did she talk football, as was our normal routine on the first day of school? No. She talked football dance.

Dance! This was going to be a new ballgame this year. And Lucy had already established herself as a blue chip player. Life has a rhythm and a season for all things. *— September 1981*

## This wanderer is always on time

Late on New Year's Eve, he drove south on 31W—heading home. Through the icy rain and the foggy night his headlights crossed a traveler bent with age.

"How far you going, old timer?"

"Not much farther tonight."

"Want a lift?"

"Yeah, boy, I could use one."

"Bad night to be out on foot, especially all alone."

"I carry this," the old man shook his razor-like sickle. "No one bothers me."

"Hope you don't mind my asking, but do you belong to some kind of religious clan or something?"

"What makes you ask?"

"Oh, I don't know; the toga, the sandals, the long white beard. Them's not the current style, ya know. Cowboy is in."

"Ach, style. I have seen them come and go. Caesar didn't mind this style."

"You knew Sid Caesar? Gosh you are old."

"About my clothes, let's say I'm on my way to a New Year's Eve party."

"Oh yeah, I forgot it was New Year's Eve. Me and the wife don't go out. She makes a ham salad, we toast some oven rolls with butter, then we watch the ball come down on TV. Maybe we drink a bottle of wine. At midnight I open the front door, turn on the front porch light and yell, 'Happy New Year, you slobs!' She tells me I'm crazy and we go to bed. That's New Year's Eve—what do you do?"

"I gotta work New Year's."

"That's rough—what are you, a fireman or something?"

"Something…"

"Well, if you go to work later tonight, I'm glad to help you get to your party early."

"I'm never early or late—always on time," the old man said as he let his heavy book drop to the car seat. "That's my trouble. I'm always on time.

You should have heard the way Joe B. Hall [former UK basketball coach] kept telling me to slow down last Saturday night. But I'm always on time, and I told Joe I don't play favorites."

"What did Joe B. say to that, old man?"

"He offered me two court-side tickets to the LSU game for a slow second half."

"You take them?"

"Nah, I couldn't. Digger Phelps is just as bad as Joe is when it comes to counting up forty minutes. I figure I know my job and I don't need any coaching from the sidelines."

"But two tickets—courtside, wow!"

"I'll be there anyhow when the time comes."

"No fooling? Wait 'til I tell the wife. I stopped to pick up a hitchhiker and he turns out to be Joe Hall's timekeeper."

"Small world, ain't it? But I keep time for lots of people. The worst of them ain't even Joe B. Hall—it's Lee Iacocca. Lee keeps begging me for more time and I keep telling him his time is up."

"Yeah, most of us figured that when we read the price tag on his Kash car."

"My mistake was taking the $1.5 billion he came up with last year. I never thought he'd get the money. Iacocca really suckered whomever he got that dough from. Wasted, all that money's wasted because Lee's time is up."

"Good for you, old man!"

"Another loudmouth is that peanut-head Jimmy Carter. Imagine him blaming his failed presidency on the times. It wasn't me who let the Shah in. Maybe next time Carter won't curse the times just before he goes skiing."

"Now pops, don't get angry…"

"Oh if you only knew, this is a rough business. Muhammad Ali kept calling me on the phone, night after night. He wanted it one more time for Larry Holmes. The ingrate. As if I hadn't given Ali enough."

"You poor guy, your life sounds miserable."

"And there's no peace. Ever since I took the Colonel to my place for dinner all we ever hear is him whistling 'My Old Kentucky Home' night after night after night."

"That's terrible."

"What's worse is I think John Lennon has talked the Colonel into doing an album. They're going to call it, 'Chicken John.'"

"Sounds like a winner to me."

"Well young fellow, this is where I get off. Thanks for the ride."

"Sure thing, pops. I'll catch you later."

"No, I'll catch you—later." *— December 1980*

# Christmas realities come knocking

I'm dreaming of a white Christmas, just like the ones you see in the Marlboro ads.

Everybody knows Christmas isn't as picture-perfect as it appears in the Marlboro ad—but we wish it were. We wish for sculptured, blue-white snow covering snug, safe, and brightly-lit ranch homes. We wish to look out the window and see Pa and Grandpa carrying home the freshly cut eight-foot spruce on horseback—with the snow falling to blanket them in a Rockwell-like sacred glow.

We wish for homes topped by perfect red-brick chimneys that curl out symmetrically-swirled slivers of rich, grey smoke; smoke rising from an unseen yet unmistakably cheery fireplace—a fireplace where tiny tots dressed in Dickensian pajamas pop corn with black iron skillets on the open fire.

We hope for—we even expect—all homes to be happy. We wish—we even demand—all fireplaces to snuggle the soft, amber glow of thick yuletide logs in their warm bellies. And above all this happiness, the stockings are hung by the chimney with care in hopes that...

It isn't like that at all. Not in real life. But oh how we wish it were so...oh how the advertising world builds up our expectations until...reality just won't do.

I grew up angry at my local priest because he wasn't as cute, as chumsy, or as cunning as Bing Crosby. Why, he wasn't even Irish!

I always thought war was mostly like the movie "White Christmas" and that all servicemen were buddies like Danny Kay. Then the Vietnam police action came and I learned for a fact that service men ain't all that grand.

As for priests being like Bing Crosby, well, any veteran of a Catholic grade school can tell you, more often the school was run by Father Archie Bunker...

There I go, even picking a cutesy TV-world bigot. As if all stupid people were as cute as Archie is...oh, don't we wish it were so.

Norman Rockwell painted pictures; he specialized in American pie. This pie was also a world I thought existed in the nice time of the 1940s and '50s. When my father came over and looked at my collection of Rockwell prints, I heard him say, "Gee, it must have been nice to live back then."

I said, "Dad, you did live back then, didn't you?"

No, my dad never saw the quaint family doctor or the honorable one-room schoolhouse of Rockwell's America. If Dad had lived with any similar such institution, it was dirtier, meaner, and dumber than the Rockwell version.

Rockwell was only an artist painting from a model's pose, not from life's reality. I still love his art; I just no longer expect it to have ever existed—except in the mind of the artist.

But oh I do wish it were so, sometimes. The same way I wish all Kentucky Fried Chicken was "finger lickin' good." The same way I wish the sweet ol' Colonel really did travel franchise to franchise making certain each store cooked according to his standards. The truth is the KFC empire produces a factory-line product, a fast food for which taste is a matter considered only after convenience and cost.

To get some really finger lickin' good bird, you need to go to a Whistle Stop or a Stone Hearth—where they take the time to cook each piece with care. And where it might cost you a penny or two more...

The Stone Hearth has the chicken but KFC has the Colonel's grandfatherly image...and as they say on Madison Avenue, sell the sizzle, not the steak.

A final word about grandfatherly images—don't we all wish our grandfather was Grandpa Walton, a wise, smiling fella who's aging gracefully, a family prophet who at the annual Christmas dinner stands to say, "My wish is for all the seasons to endlessly come and go, and that we might all be there, together, next Christmas to enjoy the secret of the giving heart..."

My grandfather would usually burp and say, "Pass the peas."

Maybe that is why we find so many people depressed on Christmas. Maybe we are all expecting Marlboro snow, Rockwell fireplaces, Bing Crosby-like priests, and Grandpa Walton to magically appear.

That's quite a tall order to fill—even for a fat, jolly old super problem-solver like Santa Claus. *— December 1980*

# Dig in—it's 'Oatmeal Weather'

It's hot, humid, and muggy weather this week. By early afternoon the Hardin County air feels like one bowl full of steaming oatmeal. And if you are like me, you have begun to look and feel like so many raisins melting into the mush. But everybody talks about the oatmeal; what is there to do?

Add water. Hot oatmeal could always be cooled by adding cold tap water. Pool water works just as well on people. Our area has several good pools and swimming holes. E-town's American Legion Park pool is open all week long with a fee of 50 cents for kid-sized raisins and a dollar for adult raisins.

Or try using your own imagination and waterworks. Garden hoses, sprinklers, or even the family bathtub (under that baseball dirt and bubble gum a kid may be hiding) can be used as water coolers.

Or add ice cream. On oatmeal days the local ice cream parlor is a good place to visit. Homemade ice cream coolers are fine, too. Our family favorite was the "Coke float kaboom." It took a bottle of Coke, a few spoons of vanilla ice cream, and some serious shaking up till…kaboom, fizzle, fun and relief from the heat.

On hot oatmeal days take a lesson from the three bears. Papa Bear took the family out for a walk while the porridge cooled. The local Greenbelt trails around town provide a wonderful way to beat the humid heat. A good strong breeze rolls in off Freeman Lake and the greenery shares its shade for picnics—so bring that porridge along.

No matter if it's hot porridge or hot oatmeal, when it's too hot to eat you have to blow on it, right? Fans and air conditioners can soothe the spirit on a hot summer day in much the same way. The rotation fan was my grandmother's machine. After she'd plug it in the fan would begin to rotate on its 180-degree mission of kindness. I recall the three grandchildren marching left, over rocking chair and coffee table, then marching right, back across coffee table and rocker just to stay in the fan's cool flow. We stayed the coolest when grandmother sat in her chair as we climbed. After all, it's hard to sweat when you're laughing to death.

Air conditioners blow during oatmeal weather. In 1965 we had the largest air conditioner in the state. My father got it free—from a going-out-of-business fish market. (Cats would come for miles when we'd start that big machine.) It was the standard 10 million BTU model.

When the air conditioner's compressor kicked in, half the neighborhood had a power failure. That summer of '65 the local power company turned to the construction of its first nuclear power plant. Nowadays the entire Spataro family sort of feels personally responsible for Three Mile Island.

Another old oatmeal trick was to put the steaming bowl in the freezer for a few minutes. With this principle in mind—my brother and I took turns sticking our heads in the icebox on hot days. We are probably the only two kids to be treated for frostbitten noses and ears during a heat wave.

Later, we modified the icebox routine. This meant keeping a complete wardrobe of clothes in the refrigerator. Nothing feels better on a hot oatmeal-like day than to put on some cool Fruit-of-the-Loom underwear that's been in the icebox for a few hours.

This "cooler closet" idea is already patented and General Electric is rushing the product into production for Father's Day. It'll make the perfect gift. So dads…keep your shorts on.

*— June 1980*

# Letting go

I drank Galliano liquore after the funeral of Larry Moore.

And just now, after the church service, clear-headed and tear-drained, I'm beginning to get it.

I get that life is a series of letting go. Of moments as well as people. We love them and we let them go. I've been reading the

Virginia Wolfe novel "Mrs. Dalloway" and noting how it's filled with one artist's love for individual moments and the certainty of each moment's passing. Wolfe understood how precious life is, and how it passes so soon, passes so soon.

Maybe only poets, a few good souls, and perhaps the saints notice life at all, understand life, and recognize it whole in moments of song, verse, and service.

I get it that such a soul named Larry Moore passed away. He was 53. A courageous family and many loyal devoted friends remember him with love. I was on the near edge of Larry's wide circle of friends. Not because he kept me there, if you knew Larry you knew his firm handshake and giving heart pulled everyone warmly, deeply, inside his life's circle.

No, I hovered on the edge of Larry's wide, kind circle because I'm still just learning what Larry understood full and well: that life is a letting go. And we love, love as best we can while we may and such love is our letting go…

I'm proud to have been a pal of Larry Moore; our final handshake came the weekend before he died. It is a private memory I cannot share but I do have one story I'll tell.

Larry and I would join mutual friends for a holiday dinner around the Christmas season. We did this for many years. From time to time my wife and I even hosted this dinner at Harmony Cove. I always liked seating myself next to Larry at dinner, because he was a champion listener. Maybe the best listener I ever knew. Seems like people these days are so darn awful busy talking they can't listen. But folks like Larry who put service above self, in a quiet, determined way, are naturally the best listeners.

One Christmas dinner at our house I offered Larry a drink of my family's favorite liqueur: Italian Galliano. I believe Larry (ever the caring guest he would not admit it) hated the stuff. Really HATED the stuff. Galliano has a distinct, almost biting, licorice flavor. My wife, refuses to even smell the stuff, says it's worse than yellow cough syrup.

But in a private moment as the other guests embraced and got ready to eat, I offered Larry a shot of yellow "cough syrup" and my Galliano story. I told him how my Father introduced me to the drink. How it was a family tradition to drink from the tall-necked regal bottle each holiday season. And how we all would pretend to have a "cold and cough" as Dad brought out the Galliano offering us all a small sip for our "Christmas cough."

Now, you have to understand this moment. It's Christmas time in Kentucky. My family is 600 miles away. Larry knows this. He is listening to my Christmas tale, hearing with his heart, as the best listeners all seem to do. His heart told Larry how, at the holidays, I would be missing my family ties, our "cough," and my quick nip of Galliano.

So whenever he was over at our house (not only at Christmas) but especially at Christmas, Larry would fake a little "cough" and ask if I'd mind if he'd join me in a little nip of Galliano for purely medicinal purposes.

Larry, I'm almost sure, hated the stuff. What he loved was an act of kindness, a ceremony, a gift he gave me, so I could share not so much a drink as a memory of distant family.

It is one of the most wonderful acts of grace I have known.

Plenty of people including his great family and his wide circle of loyal friends fondly shall remember Mr. Larry Moore.

From my edge of Larry's circle of light, especially at Christmas time upon opening a tall-necked bottle, I too shall remember and let go… *—June 2000*

## Couple giddy following swanky hotel stay

I love romance.

This Valentine's Day my wife and I pampered every romantic bone in our bodies. We went "uptown" and classy on Cupid's day. We checked into a posh luxury hotel in downtown Derbytown, Ky. I don't want to use the hotel's name in print, but just picture a seal sitting at a concert listening to the music of Bach.

I love romance.

Our stay in this music-loving seal's hotel began on Friday night when we arrived to find chocolates waiting in our suite. A split of champagne sparkled in soft candlelight. This light fell across our four-poster bed, already turned down by our unseen, yet all-knowing chambermaid.

For two days we bathed (me and the wife, not me and the maid) in a marble bath with a pedestal sink. The stylish porcelain and brass fixtures made the bathroom a hard place to leave.

A single, long-stemmed rose rested on our nightstand. We had color TV and free in-room movies. Our valet (it has a nice ring to it…"our valet") catered to our every whim and conjured up a cab to drive us to dinner.

We dined at a classic Italian (what else?) restaurant in the city. More candlelight and violin music bathed our senses. A squadron of attentive (fit, handsome, and mysterious) waiters cared for our every gastric desire. We indulged on the finest pasta dripping in the thickest, richest, red tomato sauce.

The next day (after a long, lovely night in that glorious antique four-poster bed) I treated my wife to a complete facial and makeover. She "got the works" at one of Louisville's hippest salons.

After the salon, I did for my wife what every woman wants her man to do. I took her shopping. The ground rule I set was: no looking at the price tags. If you really love it, we buy it! Buying beautiful clothes for my wife is a weakness of mine. I love the romance of seeing a new outfit come alive on her.

After she indulged me my little shopping spree we headed for her favorite part of the weekend—a gala dance in the grand ballroom of the music-loving seal's hotel. My wife loves to dance, and I love to dance with my wife in a newly-bought dancing gown.

But before dressing for the ball we popped into the "seal's" club room for a bit of the bubble. After a champagne cocktail we slipped back up to our suite. The unseen and all-knowing maid had "freshened up" our room. A new rose beamed from the nightstand. The bed was made and turned down as before.

We bathed (using the rose in the bath water) and quickly dressed for the ball. An elegant elevator whisked us up to the top floor where a 15-piece orchestra played until 1 a.m.

As we swirled and swirled on the ballroom floor we could see Louisville lit up beneath us.

Next Valentine's Day I have in mind a picnic on a deserted Jersey Shore beach. Hot coffee, warm sweaters, the roaring sea, and maybe a deli sandwich for two...

I love romance! *— February 1982*

## Reasons to exercise after the holidays

The holiday season brings Elizabethtown, as it does many towns, both happy hearts and hefty waistlines. While going through several old local diaries that described former Christmas seasons, I came across this brief account:

'Tis the week before Christmas and all through the town
Every diet is smothered with fat holiday pounds.
The stockings that hung by the chimney with care,
Are the only clothes left that most people can wear.
The children don't worry, all thin in their beds,
As memories of sugarplums dance in their heads.
But Mama in her joggers and I in old Cons,
Had just suited up to work off what we'd done.
Soon out on the street there arose such a groaning,
We jogged 'round the block all panting and moaning.
But away to the market I flew like a flash,
"I must have some junk food," said I, showing my cash.
The lure of the fat was too strong to resist,
So I purchased some Twinkies and cheese-flavored chips.
When what to my wondering eyes should appear,
But a man dressed in joggers nearby the cashier.
With his slender firm body so lively and quick
I knew in a moment it must be James Fixx.
More rapid than eagles came this jogger's great fame,
And he eyed my fat groceries and filled me with shame.
"Oh sweet rolls! Oh cupcakes! O hot apple pie!
Oh Fritos and thick shakes! Please friend, tell me why!
To the end of the block, twice around City Hall,
Now dash away! Jog away! Fat waistlines, all!"
So out on the blacktop my sneakers, they flew,
With a mouth full of Fritos (and my pockets full, too!)
And then in a twinkling I heard at my back,
The steady foot-sounds that a jogger's foot smacks.
As I drew in my head and was turning around,
Down the bypass Fix jogged in leaps and in bounds.
His eyes—how they twinkled! His breathing, so steady!
His legs strong and slender, while mine—like spaghetti!

He sprang down the bypass, to his fans gave a whistle,
And away they all ran like an ICBM missile.
But I heard him exclaim ere he jogged out of sight,
"What you lose here today, you'll gain back New Year's Night!" *— December 1979*

## Christmas play—a holiday mainstay

The Christmas play is one ritual of the season. The public school, in respect to the varying religious beliefs held by its students, focuses on the spirit of peace on Earth during a secular celebration. One parent might remember this from his child's play…

The metal cafetorium door pulls open and a cold December gust clangs it shut. Another young family pushes in. The overworked coat rack hangs under a pile of wool caps and colorful winter coats made for small people. The ground beneath the rack is a small puddle of rainwater; last year it was melted snow. Over 500 parents have come to see this year's Christmas school play.

In the packed room parents recognize neighbors with a nervous grin saying, "Me too. I'm here." The faintly uncomfortable smell of grade school is detected; the hallways, the milk trays, the paste, and the paints. Parents recall arithmetic tests taken on yellow paper, eraser-tag games, skinned knees, and stolen kisses. Soon a cloud of grown-up drugstore perfume covers the assembly with the Christmas spirit.

Carols play over the PA system. The cafetorium buzzes with chatter. Mothers wet their fingers and rub their children's faces coated with dinner's leftovers.

A small schoolgirl dressed in a white blouse and red shorts runs across the stage. Bells tied to her white gym class sneakers jingle as she runs. A hard—too loud—voice cracks in over the PA system, "Will all the fourth and fifth grade students report to the

East Wing." Parents click to attention at the announcement. They well remember this voice from above.

The girl in red and white jingles back the other way across the stage. She is joined by a similarly dressed girl exactly half her height. Their prancing steps shake the green and red paper chains looped along the stage. A parent says they're cute as reindeer.

Fathers wonder if there is time for a quick smoke in the hallway. A man in a tie walks to the stage mike and says, "Testing— one, two, three, four."

Side doors to the cafetorium bulge with nervous young actors who poke out their heads to measure the crowd. Calm teachers adorned with beautiful Christmas corsages herd them back with assurances of success.

The music teacher walks out wearing an elegant, long, black gown. She is pure grace. She turns to survey the empty stage, her back to the crowd. Later tonight she'll be hoarse from singing every song, mouthing every line, correcting every mistake.

The parents hush and the room is quiet. All eyes face the stage, lit with a single spotlight shining on a painted fireplace fire.

The play rambles on late. Finally the fifth grade boys sing, "First Snowfall" and toss wadded, white paper balls into the crowd. The house lights go up and parents find their children and file home.

Paper snowballs volley around the emptying cafetorium. The colorful Christmas chains become souvenirs to the last family out. Another Christmas play. *— December 1979*

# Thanksgiving din spoils the dinner

The house smelled rich and warm with the promise of Mother's Thanksgiving turkey. She struggled with it, lumbering from the hot oven toward the dining room. There, the main table was flanked by a collection of smaller tables donated by relatives who, being bachelors or widowers, had brought something to eat on rather than something to eat. The house flowed with family, some silently watching TV football, but most were shouting about something.

Mother thought—although shouting was not altogether unusual for her family (heaven knows it wasn't)—today's tone was hostile and that was unusual. Father pointed his pipe into Uncle Charles' chest to say bombing Iranian oil wells was not enough, if our people got hurt, so must theirs. His voice rose above a Houston Oilers' TV football fumble.

Shouting was also among the four college-age cousins present. Perhaps over the TV football, Mother thought as she piled high the homemade biscuits. No, young U of K cousin Eddie was being called a fool for studying history and being called worse for hoping to make a living TEACHING the stuff.

Grandpa kept bellowing, "A $95 electric bill. You hear me Sammy, $95! Why, we've already had to close down half the farmhouse. Might as well sell it at these rates!" Mr. Sammuels, his lifelong friend and farmhand, only shook his head.

"How can we get a loan at nowaday's rates, how?" asked young Officer Bobby Kalp. Officer Kalp and cousin Jean were newlyweds. Bobby was spending his first Thanksgiving with Jean's family. "I'd have better luck robbing some bank first."

Mother was almost finished preparing the table. Dishes and glasses sparkled empty and clean, waiting to be poured and piled upon. Already the huge pots and pans of steaming food crowded the room with a smell of abundance. She asked why the milk was left in the supermarket's plastic containers. It seems the twins had broken Grandma's fine old china pitcher while playing, "Dukes of Hazard" in the kitchen. Mother wiped the sweat from her head and bit her lip. She sent word to Father that all was ready.

Father was puffing his pipe as Uncle Charles said he'd already spent as much on fuel oil as by last Christmas day. But his family wouldn't sit in a cold house, not with baby Cindy's susceptibility to winter colds. "But I might as well be burning dollar bills instead of oil."

Everyone headed into the dining room. Mother heard the Iranian crisis come in first, followed by the gas prices, the unemployment rate, and the heating bills. The Dukes of Hazard raced in just ahead of Officer Kalp and the 15% bank interest. They all sat down shouting and complaining.

Mother screamed, "Now something may be missing—it may need a little salt," and she began to cry. *—November 1979*

## Chapter Three

# “Chuck”les

# The female neckline seems a summer thing

The female neckline seems a summer thing. It is revealed in our humid weather with hair done up and stray strands falling down, like moths fluttering near a nightlight.

At June weddings, at parties, and at proms summer necks rise from formal dresses like proud swans, bare shoulders pointing to the places where wings should be.

I like how simple and unadorned the back and necks are. Aside from an occasional tattoo this particular part of anatomy hasn't any artificial distractions: no jewels or rouge cloud and complicate the natural beauty.

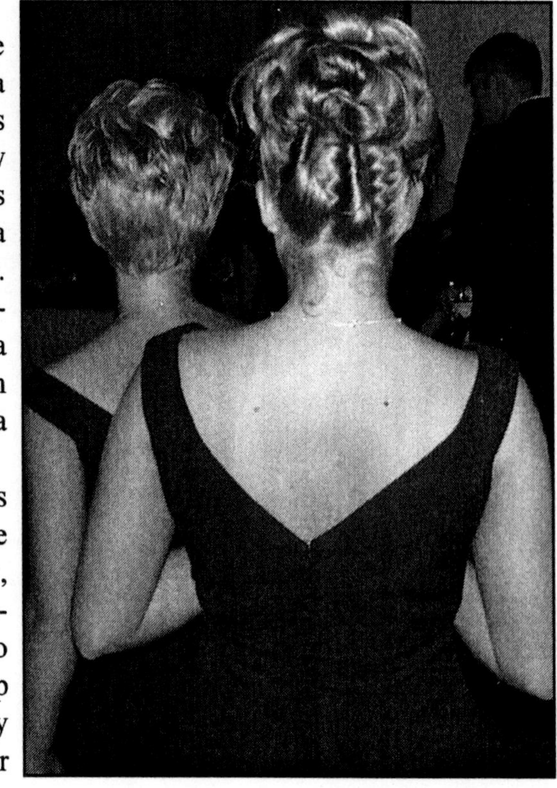

I suppose you can argue a string of pearls does slightly show around a woman's neck. This seems a bearable obstruction. And in my experience such a distraction seldom subtracts from a woman's back.

A woman's back and neckline are like summer, exact, real, and unsubtractable. No miracle bra buffs up a neck, nor any fingernail polish or contact lenses attempt to change its color. Just as summer demands a specific season, unmistakably not spring or fall, a woman's neckline takes a specific space and claims it uniquely hers.

I have a friend who takes wedding photographs for a living. He says he can tell the most beautiful women before they turn around, just from the shape of their neck, and how they carry themselves in a gown.

"Haven't you ever gone to a museum and seen some wonderful Greek statue? Doesn't it capture your attention till you find yourself watching for it to breathe? Really wonderful art makes you look at the shoulder blades to see if the stone exhales."

Eyes are supposed to be the window to the soul. But there is something too mystic about human eyes, they lack the flesh and birthmarks a human neck and back reveal. I might argue a person's back neck is more a personal fingerprint (to mix my body parts and metaphors) than eyes could ever be.

I don't know if women find the same defining beauty in a man's neckline. Necks (like summer itself?) seem somehow a feminine thing. My sister says she immediately notices a fella's hands. She asks, "Are they strong compassionate hands, or nervous flickering things?" I have heard some women say they can tell a man's heart by the shape of his hands. The writer Sherwood Anderson suggested that hands and not eyes are the true window to our soul.

For me expressive hands seem a gift shared equally among men and women. But the female neck is uniquely simple, utterly elegant, especially when rising from a formal gown on a summer's eve. *—June 2000*

# I travel, reluctantly

This morning's light shyly hugs to our lake's familiar shoreline. It lingers upon the land sparkling and clinging as if for warmth. Or perhaps safety? Or does it pause there gathering strength before its forced journey, the daylong trip in time stretching morning across our cove into the afternoon and beyond.

In mornings still closed with night I walk the lakeshore. I can understand the light's unwillingness to travel, to launch out across water and into the day. I am not one for travel either. My business as a college educator takes me out-of-town from time to time. I hate such business travel. Like the lake-light I prefer to linger near familiar shores. Today is a dreaded travel day. I must drive to Princeton, Kentucky, to some University of Kentucky Cooperative Extension agricultural outpost.

Ugh. It sounds like I am blasting off into deep space to some forlorn, isolated asteroid, a fuel depot really, and there, after landing and walking the grounds in my protective spacesuit, I'll address 12 to 15 spacey-men on my topic: whatever that is.

How I dearly hate business travel. I am like our lake's morning light before my trip. I linger at home, wandering through the house touching old and familiar things: a favorite fishing hat I've worn 1,000 times. The chipped shaving mug I rub each morning lathering while thinking through the day. The wedding photograph hanging in the hall. (Who is that fellow, a boy really, with all that hair and dumb smile shining out from his rented tuxedo?)

I smile and see my current reflection in the framed-pictured glass. I am dressed in my silly business travel suit: a navy blue jacket with button-down white shirt; a red and blue striped tie, conservative khakis pants, and dress brown loafers with tassels that jingle at my toes. My outfit might as well be the pressure suit Russian cosmonauts wear.

Carrying my briefcase to the car I feel like an old Mercury astronaut carrying his life support and cooling system in a case as he walks to the capsule. I'm on a deep space mission surely, a cannon shot to Princeton, Kentucky, and back home. I will need to spend one night in a hotel before splashing down back in my familiar lake.

I hate hotels. Their asphyxiating "clean odors" choke me. I suspect such atmospheres are not actual clean smells but some hotel maid's spray masking spills and stains. After just one day, "hotel odor" invades the pores of your skin and coats the very hairs in your nose.

Folks say a business conference is great way to: network, network, network. I'd rather meet one person a month over a long lunch than travel to a networking conference. But often, (two or three times a year is often enough) my administration urges me to "get out there and give speeches." And so I find myself in distant conference rooms full of pitchers of ice water with fine black hairs floating inside.

I give speeches because I'm asked. But almost everything I have to say could as well be easily read. My wife says just because I'd rather read a person's thoughts on paper than hear them blab it over some tin-sounding hotel PA system, doesn't mean everyone is like me.

And so I travel, reluctantly.

Driving to Princeton, Kentucky, I think of a mug, a hat, a wedding photo on the wall. These are the constant and familiar shores. My wife says I'm really a monk who's managed to find himself a willing bride. She may be right. I do confess I'm nearly a lake hermit. The place I live, Harmony Cove, offers company enough: the birds, the hermit's bride, and the way the sunlight plays its diamond dance across the lake's rolling waves. That's what I call networking. *— November 2000*

# Old explorers

Jumper, my 20-year-old cat, does not enjoy the cold as he once did. Back years ago he seemed to race round the gray months, his hot, pink tongue tasting snow and lapping ice water from the half-frozen puddles he'd bust open using a paw.

But these days he watches winter from a window box, on a pillow-ed ledge he pulls himself up on rather than leaps to. Arthritis has shortened his jump. I take good care of the old guy, give him special urinary tract food, and regular check ups with the Vet.

But he's old. And winter's cold. And old and cold don't mix.

Except on a rare occasions when the sky is a rich winter blue and there's a hint of snow flurries in the air, when limping on his hind leg he'll tap at the sliding glass porch door, pressing nose prints into the glass. And we'll go out together, explorers once again.

T. S. Eliot writes, "The old should be explorers." I think I understand what he means. The act of exploring, be it on a stroll through the backyard or sailing upon the raging sea, is more a matter of what you bring with you than with what you take home. Experience makes all the difference. For who loves a garden more: the casual youthful stroller or the veteran gardener who has seen the springs come and fall?

It has been said one takes away from a great museum in proportion to what one brings into it. Understanding the shifts and shatters in twentieth century is to understand Picasso. Failing this, then all we see is a woman with her nose misplaced.

Perhaps that is exactly what Picasso would have called the last 100 years any way?

Jumper has never said much about art (or columns now that I think of it?) but he does love these blue-skied winter days of exploration. He trots ahead of me as we pass the boats down by the lakeshore. These are boats we have passed a hundred times before. But he pauses at each one, sniffing, licking, as if each were new.

He sniffs, he smells, he scents his mark, and I follow him because I am not an explorer. I am a follower of explorers. With words, I trace footprints (sometimes paw-prints) in pathways out and try my best to write a safe journey home again. But Jumper leads on, not worrying about the return trip, a gray ball of fur and focus, he steps from boat to boat, and, then steps once again to the water's edge.

This is a stop we have come to many times before but each time he is a Columbus, a Meriwether Lewis, or a William Clark. I

sit upon an overturned boat watching as Jumper wanders, occasionally glancing back at me. He is sniffing a green bottle rolling with the waves at the water's edge. There's an old shoe. And a spaceship-shaped piece of driftwood. A dead fish. He glances back at me reporting each discovery. Jumper likes having a familiar face along on these final investigations. For my part I am happy to play Lewis to his Clark.

My lap is a place he has often slept. Fur lingers there even now, as the wind catches it and blows a few hairs across the lake. My logbook's on my lap and I'm taking notes. Suddenly I notice Jumper's ears. Each is clipped and cut from squirrel battles years and years ago. I know for a fact these tattered ears hear half of what they used to. I envy him that.

He has almost twenty years of my history inside him. Christmas trees he's attacked. Butterflies and blue birds he's chewed. And he is still the warmest foot warmer on a cold winter's night any owner could ever ask for...

But Jumper (like his owner?) has grown long in the tooth. It is a cold winter day and his paws are wet as he shivers in the breeze. But once more he dips his head into the lake and drinks: not out of thirst, but for the pleasure. —*November 2000*

# Potholes are proverbial urban pains

Some scientists claim the Alaskan polar bear is the hungriest, most cold-blooded killer in the animal kingdom.

I can't agree.

The meanest, most amoral killing creature on Earth is the Kentucky pothole.

I think it's fair to classify our potholes as living organisms. Two critical capacities a living creature must display are the consumption of nutrients and the process of reproduction.

Lord knows a Bluegrass-bred pothole can reproduce. Chuckholes on I-65 alone procreate faster than people in China. As for a pothole's ability to consume nutrients, I can testify they eat.

One ate my Toyota for breakfast this morning.

Potholes love to eat. They chew on Chevys for brunch. They dine on Dodges at lunch. Suppertime is a super time for a pothole feast of Ford Fiestas. Motorcycles and bicycles make up in-between meal snacks for our potbellied Kentucky potholes.

A typical Bluegrass pothole hibernates deep beneath the ground all winter. But a few warm February days like we've been having can awaken them. Once aroused, a pothole slips slowly to the surface (usually on I-65) looking for food.

An interesting feature about the anatomy of potholes is they are 90 percent mouth and 10 percent hungry.

And when a pothole hits topside they begin to do what potholes know best: eat and procreate and procreate and eat…

A baby hole (about the size of a hubcap) has been known to consume an entire compact-sized American-built car in one gulp. By the time a pothole's fully grown (the size of a large pizza) it's looking for 18-wheelers and Army tanks to munch on.

Another interesting feature about potholes is there is no known way to kill them. The state highway department has tried "smothering" them by pouring a temporary cold patch into their mouths.

But that doesn't kill them.

All that does is push them back beneath the surface. Once below, the critters just swim or crawl or do whatever they do and move to another location.

In fact, recent laboratory tests show that the current cold-patch filler used by the highway department actually serves as a kind of aphrodisiac to the little buggers.

Honest.

All the while road crews are stuffing potholes, they're driving the little buggers crazy with desire! Tests show that an average pothole stuffed with temporary filler will reproduce in litters of five to seven "little potholes" each...

Since my Toyota is gone, I'll have to walk to work each day. And I admit I'm mighty nervous about walking on a road full of hungry Kentucky potholes. It might be safer to move to Alaska and take my chances with the polar bears. *— February 1985*

# Trusty Ford Ranger is old enough to drive

I drive a 16-year-old truck. She's one of those "fill her up with oil and check the gas" hunks of trouble. It's a Ford Ranger, and people laugh at her a lot. They see the rust spots, the dented hood, and busted fenders; they notice her torn seat cushions, her drooping rearview mirror and they say, "Hey Cove-boy, when you gonna get yourself a new truck?"

I don't want a new truck. I just about got this one broken in. I have almost twenty years of pizza smells (leftover crust and hot peppers and such) drifting up from the crevices beneath the seat cushions. And on the dash dozens of spilled cappuccino coffees and countless Dairy Queen Blizzards scent the defroster and air conditioner when I flip the switches.

My beat up old truck has enough leftover T-shirts, socks, and torn rain ponchos to clothe me for months should my house burn down. And since I am a man who never throws away any letter or package addressed to me, I have hundreds of correspondence, from friends and foe alike, filed away in the cab. I read my mail while driving home from the post office. Then I file letters in the glove box, stuff bills under the golf balls next to the heater switches, and shove Christmas cards (dating back to 1985) under the sun visors.

I love my truck. I love that she's stuck by me so long, with little or no maintenance. You see, I'm not one of those grease monkey macho guys. About all I know how to do on a vehicle is turn the key and play the radio. It wasn't until four years ago I figured out how to pump my own gas. (Do you flip that lever up before or after you pull the trigger on the gas gun?) My truck has lasted all these years in spite of my errors and because of her own will to survive.

But time has taken its toll on the two of us. She's lost all her shocks (like me, I have no cartilage in my two bum knees.) It leaks oil and guzzles gas while good taste prevents me from mentioning what I leak and guzzle. And like me she has lost her beautiful singing voice…in the form of a damaged radio speaker from the time I drove into the lake…

I should pour a few thousand dollars into her and restore her to safe street-running mode, but I admire her "do more with less pluck." And I like how she will not go gentle into the good night. Like truck, like owner.

And hey, my truck looks good by the lake. She looks like how a truck that runs around a lake should look: crusty, worn, and as Mrs. Spataro (who refuses to ride in her) puts it, "an old catfish

rattle-trap." I resemble that remark. But put my Ranger rattletrap down in the driveway by the old weeping willow tree near Harmony Cove and she's an eternal goddess. A great old gal, a Ford you can come home to…

Me and you, my lady, me and you. —*August 2000*

# Darwin's theory applied at bus stop

Over the years our elementary schools have undergone many changes. There have been community schools, segregated schools, back-to-basics schools, and our own local back-your-superintendent-into-a-corner school. In spite of these philosophic changes, the basic process of education continues.

Fortunately we find the most critical place of learning unchanged, untouched, and eternal. I speak of the bus stop. Many citizens share the belief that more truths are discovered at the bus stop than in all the classrooms within the school district. Here are a few facts remembered from a bus stop notebook:

Fact number one: To be different is to be scorned. Picture a poor fellow standing at the bus stop with his proud new book bag hung across one shoulder. Soon he discovers only he has such a book bag. The other kids isolate him. They poke fun. They ask, "What you got in the funny suitcase, Grandpa?" and so on. Later in life this radical may grow up to run for the school board with a back-to-book-bags campaign slogan.

Bus stop notebook fact number two: Accept your chosen fate with grace. If you're the kid pushed out into the middle of the street—the one told to keep watch for the school bus—don't gripe. Later on in life you may again be chosen for some equally dangerous and thankless task like being the school board chairman for one year.

Another fact: Don't be a momma's boy. The most pitiable kid was always the one whose momma drove him (two blocks?) to the bus stop. Rain or shine momma waited and watched until Junior was safely on the bus. Once on, of course, the kids beat the stuffing out of him, day after day after day. The reason: The code of the bus stop is to eliminate the elite and eradicate the weak. If such a boy survived, he grew up to assume a position of authority in the school system such as the assistant vice administrator for transportation, food, and related services.

The facts of chivalry are also learned on bus stop mornings. The lesson is clear: Yes, it is OK to offer your finest candy bar to the prettiest girl on the bus stop but beware of the risks. If the young lady should refuse your gift, there remain only two avenues of recourse. One—to return to your friends a fool and a broken man. Or two—toss that chocolate jewel into the dirty street while staring the fair lady in the eye. Depending on which action is chosen, this boy grows up to be the assistant to the assistant vice administrator for transportation, food, and related services. Or, he could wind up as Rock Macho, winner of the Indianapolis 500.

Minding your own business is a basic bus stop fact of life. Should one kid come repeatedly to the stop with bruised lips and black eyes (after just leaving home?), don't bother him with questions. A kid's parents are his own problem. This boy grows up—only if he's lucky.

Notebook fact number six: Time waits for no one. If a sick mother who's overslept tosses the watch-like school morning routine behind schedule, tough. The school bus passes. If you dawdle over Cheerios and Captain Kangaroo too long, the school bus passes. If your sister clogs up the bathroom for two hours, it's better to hold your peace till school because the school bus passes us all.

A final fact: Don't start trouble once the bus driver pulls within view. The driver, sitting high in his yellow throne, can see every move you make. So never ask for whom the school bus horn blows—it blows for you. *—August 1980*

# You could learn from an old geezer

"I don't want to go."

"But I thought you liked visiting Uncle Chuck and Aunt Joella at Harmony Cove."

"Geezer Cove."

"Thomas, I won't have you talk that way about your Aunt and Uncle."

"Not Aunt Jo, she's cool. But Uncle Chuck, he gives me the creeps. Geezer-creeps."

"You used to like visiting him."

"Yeah, when I was seven."

"So, now you're 14, such a big shot. Since when is 14 too grown up to be nice to an Uncle?"

"Ah mom, I don't like Uncle Chuck. He lies."

"Lies?"

"Da-AAA. He still believes in Santa Claus."

"Now Tommy we've had this discussion before. Your uncle is a writer. He has imagination."

"He has a screw loose."

"Tommy I want you to turn off that stupid TV. And in ten minutes your father and I are leaving for Harmony Cove. Both you and your little sister are coming. End of story."

"Mommmm..."

"Don't mom me young man. Remember the Christmas you asked Santa for the Grateful Dead CD? Uncle Chuck was the only Geezer of the family who even knew what you were talking about. So stop this Mr. Scrooge routine right this minute. Your behavior reflects on the rest of this family. You are coming, end of story. Got it?"

"I got it. Welcome to Geezer-land."

"Ho! Ho! Ho! Welcome all. It's great to see you guys. Thanks for coming over on Christmas Eve. Ah Thomas, you've grown some more. What are you, 21? Are you married yet?"

"Very funny Uncle Chuck."

"Ah little Laura. Now at least you haven't changed, still my little niece. Go look under our tree, I think Santa left you a present here by mistake."

"Yeah Uncle Chuck, I guess when you get to be as Geezer-old as Santa is, your mind wanders..."

"What did you say Tommy? Your name is Thomas, isn't it? Or is that my name? I'm so forgetful these days. Just this morning I thought I heard the door knock. Turns out it was just my arteries hardening up. Oh Timmy or Tiny or whatever your name is, let me tell you, Christmas is a terrible season for the old..."

"Good one Uncle Chuck. Okay fine. Listen, I'm going watch some TV until it's time to go. You can tell your Christmas mumbo-jumbo to Laurie but I'm a prisoner here. That's all."

"Well, I understand. But I must have forgotten to pay the cable cause there is no TV."

"Mom! Can we go now? Uncle Chuck says his cable's dead. No TV."

"Why don't you go out by the Cove, Tommy. I'll call you in when Aunt Joella's Christmas cake is out of the oven."

"Mom! It's almost dark outside and it's getting cold."

"Thomas, do as your mother says. I mean it!"

"Dad! Mom! You guys! This STINKS! Listen. I didn't want to come in the first place. I'm going to go sit in the car! I'll be waiting so we can go home…"

"Sorry, Chuck. Tommy's been awful lately. We can't do anything with him."

"I understand Jenny. You and Donald are great parents; I guess Christmas is a hard season for the young. They just don't get it. Maybe I'll go have a chat with our doubting Tommy-boy…"

"Uh Chuck, do ya think? Maybe he should be alone for a while…till he cools off."

"Jenny, you're probably right. I'll just pop outside and see if it's snowing…"

"Oh hey, who's in that car? Is that you Tyrone?"

"Very funny Uncle Chuck. Listen man, can you just chill? I want to be alone. I'm listening to my music."

"Well that's the Christmas spirit. In excelsis Deo and all that jazz. Christmas is a time for listening, to music and such. But you'll run your dad's battery down listening to the car stereo like that. Then you and your sister will have to spend Christmas here at Harmony Cove."

"Jesus Christ!"

"Well, him too I guess."

"Listen Unk…I didn't want to come here in the first place."

"So I gathered my doubtful Tom. Since you didn't want to come here, then let's not stay."

"Huh?"

"Get out of the car and I'll show you where you can listen for Christmas. Just don't tell your mom, okay?"

"Tell her what? Hey, where we going?"

"We're gonna see Santa."

"Right. Sorry Uncle Chuck-a-roo but I'll pass."

"Sorry Tom-a-roo…no can do. Come on take the oars, we'll need them."

"We're going out on the lake at night?"

"Sure. Why, you chicken?"

"Nope. Lets go."

"That's the spirit of Christmas my young nephew Tom."

"Uncle Chuck, are you sure this was such a good idea? I mean it's dark out here. What are we really doing out here, anyway?"

"Tommy, I said I'd show you Santa Claus and I meant it."

"Okay. So where is the guy? Where's the big red suit and the jolly Ho Ho Ho's? Where's the reindeer and the sleigh? Where is your Santa Claus now Uncle Chuck? Show me!"

"He's here right now. And I'll show you him in a minute but first just listen."

"Listen?"

"Yes, just listen. There back on the shore. Can you hear your Aunt Joella's piano?"

"Hey yeah! Imagine that? We can hear the piano in your living room way out on the cove."

"Yes, Tommy. Sound travels crisp and clear as a sleigh bell on a night like this. Especially across the water."

"I can hear Laura laughing. She must have opened one of her gifts. Hey, she does sound just like a sleigh bell Uncle Chuck."

"She's a good kid, Tommy."

"I guess so. I guess…maybe I haven't been. Mom says I've been like Mr. Scrooge."

"Oh I don't know Tommy. Scrooge was taller. I think you just got confused about Christmas is all. You were thinking it was something about yourself. When it is really about loving the people around you."

"Okay you win Uncle. Let's row back. But you never showed me Santa Claus."

"Oh that. I almost forgot. The arteries dry up and the brain cells die in an old geezer like me…but I really can show you Santa Claus."

"Huh?"

"He's right here in the Cove. Look over the side. What do you see?"

"Well all I see is black…

"Go on lean way over and look. Don't worry, I got you."

"All I can see is my own face."

"That's right."

"So, that's it?"

"That's it. Merry Christmas Tommy." *—December 1998*

# Playboy kiss—a smooch to savor

On Saturday the people around Harmony Cove will gather to celebrate the Fourth of July. There's a cookout, a fishing contest for the good ol' boys to lie about all winter, and some games for the kids. I love celebrating the Fourth because it always has a "Kiss Me Twice" type of surprise in store for me.

To explain what I've said so far, I have a Billy Crystal story to tell and another story about meeting a real live Playboy Bunny once on the Fourth of July. I think maybe all this stuff is connected. I've been wrong about this kind of thing before, but, grab another cup of coffee and take a chance…

Billy Crystal is just about my favorite comedian. He seems to recognize the two lives he leads: the glitter-glamour of Hollywood and the real world of family and friends who burp a lot and tell long, boring stories at weddings and parties.

Crystal tells the story of first meeting Sophia Loren. Right after hosting one of his successful Oscar Award galas he saw Loren across a crowded room. According to Billy, Miss Loren did something he'd only fantasized about…she lifted one slender finger and beckoned Billy to "Come Hither!"

So Billy Crystal tightened his black tie and hitched up his tails and crossed the room to meet sex/symbol/movie star Sophia Loren.

"You, Billy Crystal, you are a charmer..." the Italian beauty cooed to Billy and then she took hold of his hands and said,

"Kiss me twice!"

Well, in Italy and in other European countries two quick pecks on the cheek of the face is a common greeting. But this wasn't your long-lost, distant Aunt Maria saying kiss me twice...this was, well, this was Sophia Loren.

Billy says he had already made long, passionate love to Miss Loren hundreds of times. Only she was in Rome while he was in high school. Now here she REALLY was, in person, a colleague, a potential friend, "Kiss Me Twice, you, are such a charmer..."

PECK PECK...

"Good. Bene. Billy I want you to meet someone. Federico, come meet Billy Crystal."

And Italy's most famous movie director, Federico Fellini, walked up to greet the now badly perspiring comedian.

Billy says instead of being overjoyed at meeting Sophia Loren he felt like apologizing for all those bad thoughts back in high school...

Fellini came up to Billy and said,

"Ciao, Billy Crystal. Sophia says you are a charmer, so, Kiss Me Twice..."

And that was punishment enough for the past...

All this doesn't much matter except when I went scraping around my brain for what Fourth of July story to tell you, I thought of Kimberly. Kimberly was the first genuine sex symbol I ever met in person. Back in my youth (which means before I met the Mrs.) I lived and wrote in Indianapolis. And one Fourth of July weekend I got an invitation to attend a pool party.

It was no secret that the house on the corner with the big fenced-in pool was being rented by a playboy bunny. She was Miss June/July and August...cause me and the boys in the newsroom only bought one Playboy that summer. When I told the boys I had this "pool party" invitation for the Fourth, they turned red, white, and blue/green with envy.

Well, Saturday evening promptly at seven p.m. I knocked on Miss Summer's door, hitching up my cut-off jeans and smoothing down my Indiana Pacer T-shirt.

To my surprise it turned out this was a family party. Miss June/July and August's mom, dad, and 11-year old sister were there, along with some friends from the family farm just south of town. The "pool" part was in quotes on my invitation because it was a billiards party. I played two rounds of eight ball with Miss Summer's 11-year old sister before my hostess could say hello...

My hostess was busy, dutiful, and quite a charmer. She had on the shortest shorts (back in the seventies we called such things "hot pants") I'd ever seen, except for those she almost wore in her photo spread. When she finally got around to welcoming me she said,

"Hi, you're the columnist from down the block, aren't you?"

I smiled my best Humphrey Bogart smile and said, "Sure, sure, that's me. I've been waiting to say..."

"This is great!" Miss June/July/August said, grabbing my hand and dragging me to the kitchen.

"I have someone who's dying to meet you!"

Okay I thought. Maybe Miss September/October/November needs cheering up...I'll work my way back up the calendar...

"Daddy, this is the newspaper guy you asked me to invite. Charlie, isn't it?" It was looking like a Charlie Brown rather than a Humphrey Bogart night.

"Daddy, this is Charlie. Charlie, meet Daddy."

"Glad to meet you son. (Fat handshake) I read your stories all the time. My little (what's little?) girl told me you and she were practically neighbors. So I asked her to see if you'd drop by...I want to tell you about the time I led my high school team to the state championships. I bet your readers will get a kick out of this! Hey, can I get you some more cole slaw?"

I was just glad he didn't ask me to kiss him twice...

*—July 1998*

# Chuck shuns technology

Here at Harmony Cove, Kentucky, it's a raw March Sunday, the first Sunday in spring. My wife's daffodils have bloomed on schedule but their golden buckets droop sorry shoulders in the wind off the lake. There is a bit of blue in the sky and some sun today but March is more winter than it is spring.

Seeing frost slip across the water covering the rowboats and canoe boats huddled along shore, I'm thinking of tomorrow's Academy Awards and technology. The current movie house record breaker is "Titanic." I imagine "Titanic" will snatch an Oscar or two Monday night as Billy Crystal keeps millions smiling at our own absorption with excess. This blockbuster "Titanic" is all about technology.

I'm cautious about technology.

We have to pause now for my wife to stop laughing. Mrs. Spataro knows I'm sort of a low-tech guy. She says my idea of tapping into technology is putting the toilet paper on a spool. Well, she might be right. The movie "Titanic" spins a tale about man's faith in machines. I just don't believe in the idols of technology.

Don't get me wrong, some technology's great. Take cars. I love cars. I love how the new Fords are kicking the NASCAR butts off those Chevy stock cars these days. But tell me, do the showroom versions of Taurus's really need electric windows and electric butt-warmer seats?

And TV remotes. I hate them. I firmly believe TV remotes have ruined the sanctity of the American nuclear family. What is the incentive to stay married if you no longer need your wife to get up and change channels?

And VCRs. If VCRs aren't the Devil's tool, I don't know what is. It is against the natural order of things to be able to save up episodes of "Seinfeld" and "Friends" for watching on Sunday afternoon. I think this "wrong-time" TV viewing caused the greenhouse effect and the evaporation of our ozone. You could look it up. Global warming didn't hit our planet until Radio Shack and Wal-Mart begin carrying remote controls.

Leaf blowers—they drive me crazy. They make an inhuman sound, a sort of whi-I-I-I-ne that is really the cause of El Nino. Hey mister, GET A RAKE! They sell them for $5.99 at any Super/Grocery/Store.

Which reminds me, I hate these Superstores. Hello! All I want from my grocery store is GROCERIES. Not everything you'd also find at Macy's Dept. Store. When I want to buy a wigit for my whatsit, I'll go to a wigit/whatsit store. But, oh, the Superstore's save time you say. Save time for what? So you can rush home to use the electric garage door opener (another remote) to park the car so you can get out the supercharged power hedge clippers and trim the shrubs...

In "Titanic," Director John Cameron tells a tale of how frail man's technology can be. The Titanic was, at this century's start, our greatest technological accomplishment, and unmistakably unsinkable. By the movie's end Cameron shows us that only man's spirit and the power of human love are unsinkable.

Now, if Mrs. S. and I had been on the "Titanic" we would have survived. Maybe everybody would have. My skepticism in technology would have forced me to stay in the pilothouse with my eyes glued to binoculars searching for icebergs.

It is a bit ironic that Cameron uses all of our century's high-tech, dream-making wizardry to share such a very low-tech message. I really don't think this movie needed all the gazillions it spent on special effects. The secret to "Titanic's" titanic box-office appeal is the love between teen throb Leonardo DiCaprio and that jewel of the sea, Miss Kate Winslet.

The two teenage girls in front of me cried and cried. They didn't weep for the drowned craftsmanship of the ships well-designed engines. They didn't sob uncontrollably at the rupture of "Titanic's" sleek hull. One teen turned to the other and said, "She must be so cold..." "She" being Miss Winslet, not the Titanic.

"Titanic" is a wonderful movie. I've seen it once and may take the Mrs. to see it again. Well I will, as soon as she finds the TV remote. *— March 1998*

# Bedroom window diddle

My bedroom window looks out upon another world. A winter woods where the trees are so black and the new fallen snow is so white that together they look like musical notes, sketched by

a quill pen on rough parchment. Nearly waking, these notes conspire to play a nursery rhyme, keeping me asleep. I hear, hey diddle diddle, a cat and a fiddle and when the cow jumps over the moon I can't recall if I've ever seen a window so wonderful. With a view of snow so white, trees so black, or a world so beautiful.

I know life's not just black and white. But sometimes I wish and dream it were. I wish and dream as it snows, and then, out my window the morning light bounces from black tree trunk to white, snow-filled limb and I laugh to see such a sight. Together the morning's light and the window's view make music like a silent snow, falling swish, in the notes we all dream we hear as we wake.

Almost waking, I think I want to put on boots and gloves and roam these woods. But I can never decide. Footprints ruin a fresh snow. Will waking steps break the brilliant blacks and whites into grays and slushy hues? But safe in this moment, out the bedroom window my dream is frozen and whole, a hearth of winter unbroken by human heat.

This is the temporary but perfect world out my bedroom window. Made of black and white notes on a snowy tree. Perhaps upon some distant moons a more permanent purity exists. But not on our earth's moon. On our moon tiny boot prints crowd the surface. Messy astronaut prints. Humans can be such tourists. And I don't wish to be a tourist on this snowy day.

Some say all our dreams go to the moon to stay. Waking, I want to put on two boots, two gloves, and enter the quill's music, moon walking. But I fear that once outside, my boots will smudge the snow. That's one small step for man; one giant shriek of mankind.

Is it better to wait inside, nose smudged to the looking glass and dream?

Or are we all explorers in pressure suits? All of us dressed in boots, gloves, and thick goose-quilted parka pressure suits. Bound to go like pudgy space kids where no man's gone before? Stepping deeper and deeper into the woods as our dials dip, the tanks emptying, and halfway out is all we can hope to travel. Because beyond that would leave no consumables left for coming back.

I am an astronaut whose thick oxygen tanks smell like bacon cooking in the kitchen. My wife is calling me to breakfast. She says I have to get up and shovel the driveway soon. I cover my space helmet with the pillow and turn over to dream.

My space helmet has a tune inside it. Musical notes which repeat in a singing-song…"Hey diddle diddle that cat plays a sweet fiddle and the cow jumped over the moon." But then my wife shouts, "Charles, if you don't come now, I'll feed it to the cats." And the dish runs away with the spoon. *— January 2001*

## Turning 30 has its wrinkles

Pardon me if I'm grouchy. I don't often get so out of sorts, but today there's good reason. My dumb calendar seems to insist that I'm 30.

Thirty years old. The milestone of middle age. A stage also somewhat unkindly referred to as the big three-oh. How could this be happening to me? I mean, how can I possibly be 30? I still haven't pitched in the World Series, or had my picture on the cover of "Time."

How can I be 30 if I haven't sailed around the world in my boat? Listen to me you stupid calendar, I don't even own a boat yet! How can I be 30?

Thirty. It's a word that rhymes with dirty. As in dirty deal and dirty shame and how in the world can I be 30? It's just a dirty trick, that's all. I had plans, dreams to fulfill before the big three-oh. But how do you tell a know-it-all calendar to shut up?

Thirty. Am I really 30? I guess so. The arithmetic points in that direction. Born in 1953, sweet sixteened in 1969, and now sour thirtied by 1983. I suppose I knew it would happen; I just never expected it would happen so darn soon.

All right you smart aleck Snoopy calendar, I admit it! You're right. I'm not 29 anymore. But weren't we going to be richer by 30? And didn't we plan on owning a plane (not to mention a boat) by now? And how come if experience is the great teacher, I'm not any smarter now that it's the big three-oh?

Yeah, you can't explain it to me, can you? You're a great one for telling us the what and when of each day, but you get awful quiet during the whys. Why am I 30 if I haven't found a cure for cancer or climbed Mt. Everest? How should I feel about this 30-year-old stuff?

How do I feel? Well one thing I can tell you is I don't enjoy the shower as much as I used to. Years ago, I sang in the shower. Now I find it tough to carry a tune while watching the water carrying away my once thick, curly hair.

And it's getting harder and harder to count my toes in the shower. Why? You don't know why, do you, Mr. Know-It-All Calendar? Maybe because this big three-oh belly keeps casting a shadow that wasn't there 10 years ago.

If things don't change soon, I'll be a 31-year-old man who can take a shower without getting his feet wet…

How does it feel turning thrice 10? Well calendar, old pal, I'll tell you. You know about seasons, right? Every year has four good seasons. Being 30 is like being September. You don't know if you're summer or fall, adolescent or adult.

My head says I'm full-grown but my heart thinks not. My head says I vote, I pay taxes, I work and contribute to society, but my heart still wants to go trick-or-treating on Halloween. And I just don't know which to trust.

To make matters even worse, there's that thing we chanted back when I was a teenager. You remember it, don't you Mr. Calendar? We chanted it and even believed it a little bit, too. "Never trust anyone over 30?"

So, how does it feel to be turning the big three-oh? I feel like a grouchy character from an old Pogo cartoon. I have met the enemy and he is me. *—July 1983*

# Soft contacts are for wimps

I wear contact lenses. The real kind—hard lenses. If it can be said that real men don't eat quiche, then nor do they coddle down with soft contact lenses.

Soft lenses are for sissies. People who own soft lenses sleep with footy pajamas. They drink instant coffee instead of home brewed. And, Richard Simmons is their idea of a movie star.

A hard lens man like me is tough. We're sort of like the Marlboro Man. Sure we know hard lenses hurt more, but it takes a hard lens to make a hard man…

Anyway, vanity's price is often pain. Don't tell me those sexy spiked heels the ladies wear feel comfortable. And sausage-skin tight jeans we guys put on got to grab down where the sun don't shine. Still, people endure this pain—and for what?

For vanity's sake. I'm willing to admit to a slight vain streak. My wife says if my streak were any wider, I'd look like a 6 foot 2 inch skunk. But I figure I have an excuse.

I'm in show biz. I've got my sexy image to maintain. All of us columnists bear the same burden. We're sex symbols (except for Richard Simmons, who doesn't count…)

Being a show biz sex symbol forces me to keep my fans in mind. Just as Burt Reynolds never goes out without a close clean shave, I never go out without my contact lenses. My hard contacts—the kind real men wear.

Me and Burt suffer our inconveniences for the little people, the average Mr. and Mrs. America who spend that hard-earned quarter for a newspaper. To them we're a couple of heroes, so who are we to smash the dream?

Suppose the word got out that I wore sissy lenses? Why, there'd be an outbreak of confusion among the readership. Sacks of mail demanding that I "say it ain't so" will pour into the newspaper office.

If people thought I was soft enough to endorse sissy lenses, then they might think being soft was OK. Millions of joggers would stop running at dawn. People might sleep late on Sundays and skip church. The volunteer Army's recruit rate would plunge and our entire nation's productivity would plummet to Depression-day levels.

No, I love my country too much to let her down. I plan to continue my efforts to keep back the commie invasion. I intend to set my standards high and strive to be the tough-as-nails hard contact man the world expects me to be.

But I'm only human. I admit it would be nice to be soft. I could put these sissy lenses in and forget about the world for a week. That week I'd wear footy pajamas all day and eat quiche in bed. I'd smoke Virginia Slims and drink Mello Yello.

Yes, I'm tempted. These hard lenses hurt. I tell you that at 6 a.m. after an all-night session of beer drinking and girl-chasing with my pal Burt, hard contacts really hurt. They feel like dry potato chips going into my eyeballs.

But I hang tough, like a real man, and stick the buggers in. I'll never change. I'll always be a hard contact guy. I've really got no other choice. You see, I lost my glasses trying to save my rubber ducky from drowning in the tub. *—January 1983*

# It's voting day-o!

Thank goodness it's over. This election was about as easy to stomach as drinking a flat can of soda after somebody dumped their cigarette ash inside. The key images here are: flat, canned, sugary, vulgar, and dumped-upon.

But I voted. Before I did, I went for a long walk on election eve. Hundreds of homes glowed with the blue TV light of indecision. Or was it the blue light of frustration? Of hopelessness? The still November air carried a tired smell, the mournful, wasted scent of burning leaves and twilight fires.

There was also a sad song in the night—a mournful blues song being sung. And with apologies to Harry Belafonte, I'd like to recreate the mood of a nation on its election eve by rewriting the words to this song.

"Day-o, de-oh-day de-oh-day de-oh-day voting day-ay-ay-o. Daylight come and I want to stay home.

I work all day cause inflation's fun,
Daylight come and three candidates run.
Three men tell me where they are from,
Bad news is that I got to choose one.

Bad-o, news-is-bad, news-is-bad, I'm so sad-ad-o, daylight come and I got to choose one.

Hey Mr. Anchorman, come tally me analysis.
Daylight come and I wonder who run?
Car-ter, Rea-gan, Ander-son,
Daylight come, bring still the same bums.

Pray-o, me-say-pray, me-say-pray, me-say-pray Lord help next day-ay-o,

Daylight come I pray someone else runs.
Hey Mr. Pollsterman, come poll me random survey,
Daylight come and me need to go vote,
One poll, two poll, three poll….hunch!
Reagan win putting Jimmy out to lunch.
Hey Mr. American come tally your bananas,
Jimmy, John, and Ron quite a bunch.
Jim's mean, John dreams, Ron not young
(When daylight come he forget what he done.)
Ron acts, Jim hacks, and John can't win but
He needs a lot of money cause the debt he is in.
John thinks, Ron winks, and Jimmy's quite precise
If he'd go back to Georgia, that sure would be nice.
Come Mr. American and tally your bananas
Daylight come and you must go to vote.

Day-o, de-oh-day, de-oh-day, de-oh-day voting day-ay-ay-o, daylight come and me want to stay hommmmmmmmmmmmme."

The last sad notes hung in the dark night sky. If tomorrow was election day, so be it. America would sing the blues tonight and vote the blahs tomorrow. In the booth America would be humming a different song, a song just as sad and just as sweet.

"Plop, plop, fizz, fizz, oh what a relief this is."

*— November 1980*

# God alone could save Mr. Gorsky

We all remember the famous words Neil Armstrong uttered July 20, 1969, upon slipping off the lunar module ladder into the ancient dust soil of the moon. "That's one small step for man, one giant leap for mankind." I vividly recall watching on our black and white TV at home, watching and thinking God Alone stood there with Armstrong.

I worried sick over that flight. Walter Cronkite, with his sad old owl face, didn't help much. He kept reminding us there were no back-up systems for the lunar ascent engine. Only one chance existed for firing the rocket into a safe lunar orbit.

So I sat glued to the TV screen sweating bullets and worrying. I worried about the engines misfiring. I worried we were trespassing past some locked door, a mystery, a threshold mankind, perhaps, should not traverse. I prayed for Armstrong's safety and for the lives of all the Apollo 11 crew. I just knew the ascent engine (as that sad owl kept hooting nooo…noooo back up systems) would miss-fire, leaving Armstrong and his crewmate to wait in darkest space with God Alone.

I was a very strange teenage boy.

Well, now I've learned another interesting story about this historic event. Had I known this story about Neil Armstrong I would have been able to laugh a little during the tense moments before lift off. I don't know if what I'm about to relate to you is true, but if it isn't, it ought to be.

It seems that just before Armstrong re-entered the Lunar Lander he made an off-the-cuff remark, "Good luck, Mr. Gorsky." My friend tells me the people at NASA thought it was a casual remark relating to some Soviet Cosmonaut acquaintance of Armstrong. But they checked and there was no Cosmonaut Gorsky on record.

So what could Armstrong's cryptic message mean?

As the years went by, and Armstrong became a University professor and NASA spokesperson, from time to time people would ask what the "Good Luck, Mr. Gorsky" statement meant, but Armstrong always ducked the question with a slight smile.

On July 5, 1995, in Tampa Bay, Florida while answering questions following a speech, a reporter brought up the 26-year-old question to Armstrong. This time the Apollo 11 commander responded. Mr. Gorsky had died, so Neil Armstrong felt he could finally answer the question.

In 1938 as a boy growing up in Ohio he was outside playing baseball with a friend. A long fly ball got smacked deep in the field and ended up in the neighbor's yard. It was the yard of Mr.

and Mrs. Gorsky. The ball rolled up next to their bedroom window and as young Armstrong bent to retrieve the ball he heard Mrs. Gorsky shouting at Mr. Gorsky.

"Sex! You want sex? YOU'LL get sex when the kid next door walks on the moon!"

I wish I had known this story just before lunar blast off. Somehow knowing Neil Armstrong's good humor was wrapped inside his pressurized spacesuit, along with the memories, faith, hopes, and dreams a human heart provided, would have helped. It would have helped a silly, worried teenage boy understand Armstrong was not so all alone after all. *—August 2000*

# Insurance agents stalk newlyweds

Why is it now when I'm happily married that everyone is so worried about my insurance coverage?

Twenty-seven bachelor years I spent without a call from an insurance agent. Not even so much as a postcard did I receive asking if I was alive this year. But three months after marriage, the general consensus is that I'm an accident ready to happen. Insurance agents now hover about me like so many buzzards above a carcass.

A telephone ring…

"Hello, Mr. Spataro, I learned from a friend of yours (some friend) that you've just married. Do you have adequate coverage?"

"Well, I'm wearing some Levi dress slacks right now."

"Quite the kidder, aren't you, Mr. S? But I take your personal security very seriously. After all, who knows how much time each of us has left?"

"George Burns?"

"Oh, you are quite the card, oh my, yes. But have you thought of fate, Mr. Spataro? The capricious whim of that woman called 'Chance.'"

"Who is this really, Howard Cosell?"

"My name is Phil Istine, and I'm talking about sudden tragedy. Like a lion's sudden rush from the bush, the crushing blows from the jawbone of an ass, or the silent strike of a black widow spider."

"I work in Elizabethtown, Ky., Mr. Istine, not in Asia."

"Would you believe food poisoning?"

"Food poisoning?"

"It's been known to happen, even in Kentucky. What's she cooking for dinner?"

"She…oh you mean my wife? Why, just some steak and mushrooms."

"I'll be right over…" Click.

Five minutes later the doorbell rings.

"I'm glad to see you're still with us, Mr. S."

"What's going on here, who do you work for anyhow?"

"Mutual of Delilah."

"I never heard of that insurance company."

"Sure you have. 'You're in good hands with Delilah.'"

"Yeah, maybe. But why are you suddenly so interested in me?"

"Statistics, for one. Statistics show that more husbands die each year than do single males."

"So?"

"So, my dear Mr. S., you have just seriously endangered your health by marrying. But the Delilah Company is here to help. May I ask you a question?"

"Sure, but my wife is due home soon. She…"

"I'll be brief. Did your wife have a big wedding shower?"

"Yes…"

"Did she get some strange presents, like large sewing scissors, a Samson-sized rolling pin, a carving set, and perhaps an 'I Hate To Cook Cookbook'?"

"Yes."

"Well Mr. S., I'm glad I got here in time. Mutual of Delilah can protect you with the total Husband Protection Plan."

"What's it cover?"

"It covers your head, Mr. Spataro. Ha ha ha ha ha! It covers death by strangulation from shrunken laundry, death from burned-out pancakes, death by heart attack after reading the credit card bill, death by…"

"Sign, you bet I'll sign. She's not going to get me. I'm not a statistic. Give me that pen of yours."

"As you wish, Mr. S…"

"Ouch, that pen pricked me!"

The front door opens.

"Honey, you're home. I feel so dizzy. Hey, what's happening to me? That pen…it must have been poisoned…"

"Mr. Istine, can you stay for dinner? I just bought some fresh steak and mushrooms."

"That happens to be my favorite dish, Mrs. Spataro."
*— July 1980*

# Office takes on life of its own

I've created a monster. A Frankenstein-like creature that I built, I'm responsible for, and who no longer needs me. It's my office.

My office is like my soul. My wisdom is on its library shelves and my dreams are postered on its walls. It even has my impossibly cluttered train of thought across the desk top. My office is a better me than I am.

For starters, my office is more respected than I am. People write to my office, not to me. They ask for my office's advice, not for my advice. Friends stop me on the street to say, "How are things at the office?" I might as well be dead.

If I did die, it would be years till the rigor mortis reached my office. Like a dead animal's twitching, the office would continue. Business might even pick up. I might be promoted.

And my local rivals would curse me, saying, "That lucky stiff still has a good office."

Certainly my departure would not affect the flow of mail. Most of my mail is addressed to my title, that is to say—to my office. It gets quite a bit of mail each day. Over the years the office has developed proper form letters for quick replies. Since many of these forms already have my signature, I could be meeting my commitments months after meeting my maker.

I don't think the appointments would suffer either. By now the walls of my office contain so much of my fancy (postcards, pictures, and snapshots of the family) that visitors would still get an impression of me. My clients could come in, sit down, talk over matters while addressing my office chair. The spirit of Spataro is there now. It left my body months ago.

Much like Dr. Frankenstein, I'm frightened by my creation. It intimidates me. I dress to please my office. I cut my hair and choose my friends to meet its expectations. I tell it when I'm coming in, and where I'm going out. I ask it for vacations.

I've been in business so long that I no longer can remember the statistics of my work. This is where the office exerts its greatest power over me. It has all that information locked up in those damn files. If I need to answer a question, I have to go ask it. Then I must get down on my knees and beg the files for information. Oh how I must grovel to obtain the proper facts for the annual report.

And I don't like its friends. Yes, by now the office has made several close friendships of its own choosing. I'm expected to be civil and entertain its guests. I give them coffee. I drink coffee with them. I don't even like coffee.

My office gets invited out quite a lot. It's on all the right lists: for workshops, for town meetings, for civic clubs. Most of the time the office is too busy to attend itself, so it sends me in its place. I do my best, but the disappointment is always plainly written on the host's face. I am bid goodnight with a polite, "Give my regards to your office."

This past holiday I didn't even get invited to the office party. I sat home alone, a man without his soul.

I am not jealous, and do not mean to suggest that the office hasn't earned its respect. It is a good office. I know that. My boss often comments, "that office puts out a lot of work." I just wish I hadn't given it so much of myself. I wish there was still some of me left for me.

If I do die and go to heaven, St. Peter is going to stop me and ask me for my soul. I'll just have to tell him the truth.

I gave at the office. *—July 1980*

*Chapter Four*

# For the Love of the Game

# Thwack

I know I'm in bed waking. I know that this is just a dream. But we dream on anyway, don't we?

I have been to the very spot where I catch my dream. It's 30 minutes around the lake, a ground rule-double from my house. I have stood with reality's eye staring down at my dream's view. It is pretty much as I've dreamt it. The woods are more real, the shore has a fisherman's bait can or two which never seems to make my dream, but I can recognize the place. I can see home plate across the lake, and in between, I see the bridge.

My first thought almost every morning is of the bridge. This is something subconscious, probably indicting, perhaps there's even something dysfunctional going on here, but true. Maybe my brain sputters and misfires as all the synapses go snapping, like a bat cracking, until my subconscious vaguely explains waking to my conscious with a bridge.

This image is color coordinated to the seasons. In January I see a snow-covered lake with bare woods beyond. The lake is a blue-white blur as moonlight colors the morning. Frost crusts across the water and in those woods beyond, faint white snow traces show through the bare trees.

Although I always dream of the bridge, I'm not on it. I'm beyond the bridge across the lake, there upon the far shore. I am crouching, oddly perhaps, but not oddly to me. It is my baseball player's stance, the squat a catcher uses catching a pitch. I'm Yogi Berra or Johnny Bench (you National or American leaguers may choose) squatting there receiving the day. There, where woods meet water. There, away from all houses, away from all mornings' barking dogs, away from all the morning TV hosts who fill our TV screens with rude, white teeth.

I am half asleep and dreaming myself awake. Squatting like Yogi Berra or Johnny Bench, waiting for today's opening pitch. Will it be a high hard one or a slow curve? Or maybe it will be a change-up, a slider, or as the woods slowly fill with light, what?

And in between second base and home the bridge is there, a wooden synapse of another kind, connecting the mainland to the island around our cove. I wonder if that bridge did not exist, could my dreams? Second to home can be awfully far for a pitch to carry, too far without a halfway booster (perhaps a bridge) that catches a dream and pushes, boosts it on its way.

They say a major league fastball appears like this, that a Randy Johnson heater flies off the pitcher's mound almost normally at first but then halfway gone it catches fire, gets a boost, exploding 95 mph down the pike into the catcher's mitt.

Thwack.

I hear that sound waking. It could be the distant ice cracking in the cove. It might be my hand missing the alarm clock and knocking over the lamp. I am squatting, seeing the bridge, feeling the morning speeding toward me. It's coming over the middle, a high and hard one. I brace myself for the heater as I pour cold cereal into a round bowl. As I dip a silver spoon into a coffee cup, I scrape the ice off the car windshield holding up my glove, closing my eyes. I catch the morning.

Thwack. *—January 2000*

# Baseball fever—catch it

Baseball is a fever now, and people who catch it seem to get hot. The Phillies and the Royals have a fever—the Yanks and Astros had their fevers broken, a little early.

The baseball I love best is not a fever—it's more like a flavor, an ice cream flavor dripping down a sugar cone. The game I speak of is kid-baseball, a game as natural as plain vanilla with plenty of jubees on top.

Such baseball was played on hot summer days in kid-made ballparks far from Howard Cosell. We announced our own game...

"Stepping to the plate is Killer Kooselman, the dreaded home-run king," the pimple-faced Kooselman would say.

To which the pitcher might reply…

"Ladies and gentlemen, that big dummy striking out was Kooky Kooselman, batting average .089."

There were plenty of needles and jokes but very few arguments. Usually one kid had final say in all close plays. He was the designated umpire, and for us he was Rudy. Rudy was a below-average second baseman, but an average honest kid, so he did fine. Close calls went something like this:

"Out? Oh come on, Eddie, you're crazy. I was safe by a mile. What do you think, Rudy?"

"Uh, I think out also."

"You're on my team for Pete's sake Rudy, have a heart."

"I think out."

"Well you need glasses."

But he stayed out. Rudy's authority came from the kids' agreement that playing was more important than winning, surely more important than wasting time fighting over it. Rudy never made the high school team; seems they changed the agreement on him.

Vanilla baseball was everyday, like emptying garbage or eating vegetables. Girls played too because in a small neighborhood you used what and who was available to get the game in. The street became our ballpark; the girls became our teammates. We soon learned that girls were sneaky-good at sports.

"Helen? Why'd you go and pick Helen over me?"

"I wanted a good pitcher today, Arnold."

"Listen, I can pitch."

"Yeah, but Helen remembers to pitch Charlie low and away so he doesn't cream it so often."

Helen couldn't hit to save her life, but she did get the hard-hitting Charlie to pop out a lot. That's sneaky-good. Girls somehow didn't make as many mental errors as the guys did. They kept their cool under pressure situations. They also reminded us when we didn't.

"Why'd you throw to first for? You got to get the lead runner. Now they got Kooselman on second and one stupid out. Shape up, short stop, or you'll be playing right field next inning!"

Harsh words quickly passed. No gripes or grudges were carried over more than a pitch or two. The unspoken rule was to play as much baseball as the sunshine, the traffic, and the parents would let us get away with. Games went seven innings so there was a feeling of change, progress, new opportunity. We might play eight or nine games a day.

"Who won the last game?"

"You won it and you know it."

"Just checking to see if you noticed. OK, new side then, you get first pick."

"I get Helen."

"No you don't—she's my steady pitcher."

"OK, I got Larry Sorrel."

"He's not even here today."

"I know that. Wait here—I'll go get him."

Larry was that kid who hated baseball, never came out to play, but clearly was the only kid in the neighborhood who had any real baseball ability.

"No dice, you can only pick from kids here now."

"Nuts. What do you think, Rudy?"

"Pick from kids here and no steady pitcher."

We could have used Rudy at Camp David.

Rudy, Helen, and the gang—I wonder where they are today? I remember once asking Helen why she always tucked her hair up under her cap before pitching to Charlie.

"I like for him to be the one waiting till I'm good and ready."

Helen must be quite a giant-killer now. I wouldn't be a bit surprised to hear that smart Phillie caught a fever and now is part owner of some ball club out east. *— October 1980*

# Oh, the joys of stickball

Stickball season didn't get much coverage again this year.

It's probably due to the fact that there are no teams, no universally-accepted rules, and no definable season to speak of. But stickball is a game boys play each year during the hottest months of the summer. It's a game to play when baseball is impossible due to the 21-day vacation list. Stickball, you see, takes only two players.

In its purest form, stickball takes place with a pitcher, a batter, a broomstick, a tennis ball (no fuzz), and the brick wall of some grade school building. Usually a player steals some chalk (when the summer janitors aren't watching) to draw a rectangular strike zone on the wall. It must be done in chalk. Disputed pitches can often be settled by the stain on the ball or by the wall's mark.

Stickball is played in only blazing hot weather (vacation weather). It is a game of endurance. Man, stickball, wall, sweat, and sun. A batter must hit the ball a certain distance or it's an out. There are singles, doubles, and homers according to distance. Imaginary runners score runs, but not many. It is very hard to hit a tennis ball with a broomstick.

There's no curveball in this game. Just fastballs and change-ups. Most of the hits come from guessing correctly on change-ups. A batsman knows the pitcher has got to throw changes. If he doesn't save something for the last few innings, his arm will fall off. You can lose the game automatically if your arm falls off.

A pitcher worries about the burning hot sun. He worries about the dizzying loss of body fluids and he worries about his arm falling off. This makes him mad, so he throws something called the "brushback pitch." Most stickball brushback pitches hit the batter. This makes the batter worry. On a day so hot you only wear cutoffs, baseball caps, and sneakers, a tennis ball in the back stings.

The balancing factor in all this is that batters soon become pitchers. Pitchers have to remember their Old Testament. (An eye for…)

Strange as it may seem, three people participate in most stickball contests. The third (usually a younger sister) acts as ball retriever. Retrievers sit barefoot and cool in the shade of the school building. They clog up water fountain drains and let the cool water overflow on the pavement. When a long shot rips out into the parking lot, they pad wet-footed after it while the game continues with a "spare" ball.

These balls are not actual tennis balls; they are skeletons of tennis balls. A major league stickball has long been cleaned of its fuzz by tennis parents and hungry dogs. This system is known to sports writers as "the economy of sports."

In all, there are many advantages to stickball. It can be played while everyone else is on vacation. There is beauty to the solitude of an empty schoolyard interrupted by the crisp whip of ball and chalked wall. It keeps your dumb little sister busy. And at least somebody is using part of the school building during the summertime. *— September 1979*

## Baseball gear piled up on doorstep of the mind

I remember what it's like to leave your ball, bat, and glove on the doorstep. All moms in our old neighborhood shared one golden rule, that all baseball equipment stayed outside. No bats, no balls, no ash-covered sneakers came in the house. And so, my baseball equipment has remained on my mind's doorstep for 40 years. Every fall as pennant races tighten and as the World Series looms near I find myself tripping over these tools of youthful summers.

I grew up playing baseball eight hours a day, all summer long. We played on a dead-end, dirt road called Baxter Avenue, which ran between our house and the Luckman's. Mr. Luckman was a cigar-smoking, silent man whose coal furnace ash filled the potholes in the dirt road we used for center field. It always confused me how Mickey Mantle never got ash soot on his shoes and uniform playing center field for the Bronx Bombers. I just figured all center fields had ash piles, and up in the bigs, the piles must have been bigger.

Our playing field was a typical street in a blue-collar neighborhood. I grew up in a town smaller than today's Elizabethtown, maybe more what E'town must have been like back in the 1950s. We had a neighborhood gang of seven boys and two girls who worshipped four different ways (Jewish, Catholic, Baptist, and Presbyterian) but whose common religion was baseball.

We played four or five on a side: a pitcher, two infielders, and two outfielders. Special house rules made the innings more fun and more dramatic. One rule was that an "automatic home run" was awarded if you hit the Rose of Sharon bush at the end of Luckman's yard. And when your pop fly struck the telephone pole at the corner of Baxter and Liberty, it was an automatic grand slam, no matter if the bases were empty.

We used the block's youngest or worst (often the same) kid to play steady-catcher and allowed this runt an at bat whenever there was a base runner on third. Almost any kind of hit scored a runner from third, because, well, there wasn't any runt-kid playing catcher then, was there?

We were mostly New York Yankee fans and Baltimore Oriole fans who never fought over balls and strikes. Our only disputes were about who'd get to be Mickey Mantle or Brooks Robinson that day. Me, I always wanted to be Joe Pepitone, the rookie Yankee first baseman. I even bought a first baseman's glove with money from my evening paper route proving my loyalty to "Pepi."

I notice today's kids around Harmony Cove don't play pick-up ball games like we did. Today's youth belong to actual leagues and have real uniforms. They play games with umpires and they go by the official rules of baseball. I guess that's progress. Of course a kid these days might get up to bat only three or four times a game playing "town ball." In our neighborhood games, I'd bat 20 or 30 times, and I'd usually hit the grand slam telephone pole twice, before lunch.

I guess my gang never had the ambition these kids have nowadays. Today they all want more than to be major league stars. They want the big, multi-million dollar contracts Slammin' Sammy gets belting bombs in Chicago. They want the fame Big Mac garners for ripping records in St. Louie. These kids still collect bubble gum cards just like I did. But I kept my favorite Mantle and Maris cards tucked inside the sweet sweatband of my genuine Yankee cap (bought at Woolworth's) for luck. Today's kids keep their cards in pristine plastic albums tucked away in the safety deposit boxes at their parents' banks.

One kid told me he planned to liquidate his baseball card collection when he turned 40 and retire early. He said it was part of his long-range financial portfolio. Of course, most of his retirement funds he expected to accrue from trading on the stock market. Not us. The only trading we knew was when you swung at a third strike you offered the pitcher a baseball card for another try.

"Hey Linda, IF you give me one more swing, I'll give ya my Yogi Berra card!"

"Toss in a Willie Mays and I might even let you hit one, Chucky Boy."

Somehow, even as eight-year-olds, we knew baseball would never get any better than what it was on Baxter Avenue. We'd play 22 innings before lunchtime and then all run home, pausing to kick off our ash-covered sneakers at the doorstep. Every night Mr. Luckman (who looked like Mr. Wilson from the Dennis the Menace comic) would carry out a kettle of ash. Dumping his ash in center field, he'd yell at us "to choke up more on the bat, just meet the ball kid, ya don't all need to be Babe Ruth!" Then he'd grunt and flick the inch-long ash from his stubby cigar into the pile he'd just dumped. He always mumbled how kids didn't appreciate the beauty of baseball.

Funny, but except for his cigar, I guess I've turned into Mr. Luckman. If he were here today, he'd remind me how lucky I was to play ball where his Rose of Sharon home run bush grew, and how baseball on Baxter Avenue wasn't any bush league. For baseball, wherever it is played, when played with the heart, is big league ball. *— September 1999*

# Dream caps

In my pick for best movie of the year, "The Cider House Rules," actor Michael Cain plays a poet-philosopher, abortion-performing, doctor-caretaker of orphans. Cain gives a wonderful, Oscar-worthy performance. The whole movie makes you laugh, cry, hope, hate, and did I say, cry? But there is one scene I most recall.

Too weary from his duties to sleep, the aging doctor puts a surgical mask to his face and pours a drop of ether upon it inducing a dream state. Seeing this, I thought back to my youth as a boy on baseball fields. There, on those backyard ball fields supported by friends, boys and girls alike, we played for whole days not innings. And there on those fields we'd put on our own dream-inducing masks.

Exhausted from our play, we'd lie on the grass covering our faces with sweat-soaked baseball caps, smelling the past day. Smelling the home runs and smoothly played catches of the day. From inside those caps actions both real and imagined passed before our eyes. I'd see the ground rule double that got stuck in Mr. Luckmans' apple tree. I'd feel and smell the slide I'd made at third (or would have made if I hadn't been tagged at second).

From beneath those caps we could replay any play, tag any base, and touch any dream. I could become Joe Pepitone for one at bat, Brooks Robinson the next. Chasing a high pop fly I was Willie Mays going back, glove in a basket-catch position. Diving for a hopeless sinking line drive to right, I'd become Mets rookie Ron Swaboda. And there inside my cap would be my manager, Casey Stengel, explaining to the press, "Whaddaya mean it's St. Patrick's day and the Mets ain't got on no green? We got Swoboda, and he's plenty green."

Behind my cap I most often became Lawrence "Yogi' Berra. I identified with the Italian backstop and wore his number eight crayoned onto the back of my white T-shirt. Yogi and I were both awkward and unsightly enough that while stepping up to bat our own teammates yelled, "Hey Berra (Spataro) you're too ugly to play baseball." To which Spataro (Berra) replied, "Oh yeah? Well, I don't hit with my face," and with a little cap-magic I'd promptly smack a double off Luckman's apple tree.

Then twisting my cap over my face I'd smile and become the immortal Babe Ruth, beer belly and all. The press would be there asking me, "Hey Babe, your new contract from the Yankees makes you better paid than the President of the United States! What do you say about that?" "Well fellas," I'd say from beneath my cap, "maybe I deserve more dough. I had a better year than he did."

Masked behind a cap I could be Phil Niekro floating a knuckler at Mike Schmidt. Or I'd be DiMaggio hitting in 56 straight. My friend Glen would be Joe Morgan double stitching his grip, or

Ty Cobb stealing home. Sometimes we'd lie there till dark and just saying names through our caps. Say Whitey Ford and inside our caps a number 16 in pinstripes would appear. Say Warren Spahn and here came a big-nosed balding lefty with a "M" on his cap tossing his 363 win.

I haven't played a baseball game in thirty years. People tell me I've grown to look a lot like Warren Spahn did in his final few seasons. Which, if you knew how Spahnie looked, you'd understand isn't high praise at all. I still buy a new baseball cap every spring. I wear the cap mowing the grass, washing the car, and while traveling places here and there in my adult life.

Lots of guys my age wear caps, so I pass unnoticed among the John Deere and Big Blue toppers. But when I see an old bald guy like me with a Cincinnati Reds cap or Pittsburgh Pirate hat, I wonder if, every now and then, he does what I do. What I do is doze off on the recliner out in the garden. I'll tell the Mrs. not to wake me for an hour.

And I'll pull my ball cap up over my face seemingly blocking out the sun. And then I suck in a good deep breath, smelling the spring ether and the Hyacinths in bloom. And dream.
— *March 2000*

# House rules rule in the rec room

Where's the most fun you ever had playing games? For me, it's the Ping-Pong room in the old basement we've fixed up here at Harmony Cove. The room's not much. There's a wall with a few molding photos of me in Boy Scout and baseball uniforms. On another wall hangs the red and black flag my wife proudly carried for the East Hardin High School band. The windows have some curtains we found at Wal-Mart and through those windows you can see silent fishing boats floating like bobbers in the cove.

We play lazy, loafing Ping-Pong, not the serious skilled table tennis you see during the Olympics. This is true partly due to the geography of the basement. The heating air ducts hang so low over the Ping-Pong table that lob shots are completely impossible. The poor overhead lighting makes only glow-orange balls useable. So far the six Ping-Pong balls we got with the table have dwindled to four survivors. I think one ball rolled off and was eaten by the furnace. The bloated look of our cat Jumper makes me worry where the other ball's gone.

But each game is an adventure. My wife's game is built around placement rather than power. She yells some old Rebeleer band cry when we get a rally going. If we hit the day-glow ball over four strokes she starts laughing. And should one of us "accidentally" hit the very white edge on a critical shot, she collapses in laughter.

We play silly "house" rules dictating the ball's being in play off the walls and air ducts. Anytime a cat jumps on the table the person on the cat's side may choose to suspend play or to continue the point. Plus the server gets to say if the next five points are played with or without the use of Ping-Pong paddles. My wife's bare-knuckle backhand is tough to return using just my fleshy hand for a paddle.

I have learned the only sure way to defeat my wife is to play country music on the old stereo down there. She'll get to singing with Trisha Yearwood ("There Goes My Baby...") and soon loses concentration long enough for me to slip in a spin serve.

Her secret for disrupting my game is food. (Most of my trophies down in the game room basement are for pie eating contests.) She'll pop popcorn or bake cookies and strategically place the food bowl near the Ping-Pong table—but not too near. When I step away to grab a handful of cookies she quick-serves me. Timing is everything in sports.

The only other time and place I've had much joy playing games was on the sandlot softball field my gang used when I was a kid. Our block had about nine kids who loved softball and we met without parents, without T-shirts or sponsors and played softball for hours and hours every summer's day.

The field was really a dirt and gravel road which dead-ended into a place the neighborhood dumped coal ash from their furnaces during winter. Nine kids, four on one side and five on the other, played with a ball held together by mostly black electrical tape.

We had seven guys and two girls who shared each other's gloves and bats and ball caps. The outfielders got to wear the caps to shade their eyes on the pop flies. One girl's hair always made my cap smell like raspberry. I didn't mind. She was sort of pretty and she contributed a genuine Louisville Slugger bat with Joe Pepitone's name on it. I was always a sucker for any woman who liked Joe Pepitone.

Sometimes when the other girl's piano recital was coming up, we had her as "steady pitcher" on account of her mother's belief that batting caused a girl's naturally flexible fingers to stiffen...like a boy's.

On hot summer days we brought tin buckets with ice from the soda pop shop down the block. My best friend got fruit from his dad's deli and dropped in cut slices of peach or apple to flavor the water bucket. We all drank straight from the bucket—what would the county health department say about that today?

The water bucket also served as first base; don't ask me why. I know that if you hit a single you got to hold the bucket in your arms like Wimbledon's Cup and sip some rich, cool water. It was sort of an unwritten rule you had to "accidentally" catch a piece of fruit in your mouth as you gobbled down a drink, eating the fruit on purpose would be sort of stealing from the other eight ball players. Stealing wasn't allowed, not on the base paths and not from the base-buckets either.

The part I liked best about our softball game was keeping score. We didn't. What we did was keep track of how many runs the defense could hold the offense to before getting three outs. We never kept a running score. Every inning was a new challenge. We played eight innings and switched teams. I don't know why. Eight just worked out right, gave every kid enough at bats and enough tries at the fruit bucket at first. So eight innings it was.

We all knew this brand of ball was not what they played in the "official" little leagues in town. Three of our gang even played regular "league ball" but it was never mentioned. Like piano lessons or an early morning paper route, they did it but it was not fun. It was a task, a chore, almost like a job. What we did with our lopsided-taped softball and liquid first base was the fun.

Harmony Cove Ping-Pong is the same kind of fun. Like the softball gang did, my wife and I make up new "house rules" as we go. Last night I learned any ball hit off a cat's backside was still in play if the cat meows. No meow meant it's a dead ball and the point must be replayed. This was my wife's rule.

"Wait a minute," I said. "We never played the meow rule before."

"We have now!" said my wife, smacking a hard spin serve off the cat.

"Aw, you can't do that," I said. "You already have an unfair advantage!"

"What's that?" asked Mrs. S.

"Your fingers are naturally more flexible than mine."

*— August 1998*

# Baseball excuses run out eventually

Baseball the beautiful. Our national pastime, the great summer's game. Baseball is a tradition molded in a diamond of earth set upon a field of green. Baseball is a bat, a ball, a glove, and a man's made-to-order excuse for not working around the home on weekends.

Wives know. They've been hearing the same excuse from husbands ever since Mr. Doubleday created the game way back in 1838. "Gee honey, I'd love to help you clean out the garage, but there's a ballgame today."

Baseball. A simple game, really. A game invented by a husband to help get husbands everywhere out of weekend work. Any wife will tell you baseball is called our national pastime because for more than 100 years men have used it to pass time spouses had planned for household chores.

Football could never be the national pastime. Football is played during winter when the cold is its own excuse. Were there to be a football strike this season (imagine that, can you?) men could always say, "Aw honey, it's too cold to clean out the garage."

But in the summertime, a woman's fancy turns to painting the front porch. At such times, baseball is a man's only excuse to keep the living easy.

So far, I've managed to kcep the strike a secret from my wife. However, last Saturday she came into the TV room with the dreaded job jar in her hands. I froze—but quickly recovered.

"Aw honey, don't bring that jar in here now, there's a game about to start." Luckily she turned and was gone before the tube squealed out the theme from a "Father Knows Best" rerun.

Another close call happened on Sunday. She wanted to go visit our in-laws. Luckily this time ESPN (a husband's Easy Sports Pardon Network) was broadcasting an NCAA ballgame. Saved by the amateurs. But my wife was getting closer to the truth all the time.

Driving to work Monday morning she overheard big-mouth Howard Cosell (who else?) blabbing about the tragically ubiquitous baseball strike. I quickly changed the radio station but she had caught it...

"What strike?" she asked.

"Aw, honey, heh, heh, heh," I sweated, "you know Howard Cosell. He's always talking nonsense."

"I heard him say there was a baseball strike."

"Sure, uh, heh, heh, (more sweat) baseball has lots of strikes. Lots of balls. Lots of hits...hey, isn't that a new hairdo you're wearing?"

"Mr. Cosell was saying something about there being no baseball this Fourth of July weekend, Charles."

"He meant that there will be no home games this weekend, dearest."

"Now Charles, if the Reds go play Houston, even then somebody has to be the home team…"

"Well not really. You know how it is with these new ball parks, the night games, and the free agent draft—it's so complicated even I don't understand it all."

"If you didn't have a ballgame to watch, you could fix that leaky faucet in our basement."

"But dearest, I'm telling you there ARE games—I mean—how could there be a Fourth of July without baseball? Don't I always watch a double-header on the Fourth?"

"Yes dear, I'm sorry I argued with you."

"Aw, that's OK honey, I love you…"

"And I love you too. In fact, to make it up to you, I want to give you a treat. Why not get us both tickets to see the Reds play their double-header this weekend, my treat."

"Uhhh…"

"What's the matter, dear? I thought you loved to go see a ballgame. Now I'm agreeing to go with you."

"But dearest, I hadn't planned on doing so much traveling this weekend."

"Oh Charles, you know it's not far to Cincinnati."

"Yes, but Cincinnati is not where the closest baseball game will be played this weekend."

"Where, then?"

"I think in Tokyo, Japan." *—July 1981*

# Strike! Everyone else does!

Coal miners can. Teachers, policemen, and firemen can—so why can't baseball players strike?

Strikes and baseball go together hand and glove. They're like hot dogs and mustard, pizza and beer, like Mantle and Maris. It's only natural to think of strikes when you're talkin' baseball.

My own baseball career was filled with strikes. I had more strikes than any other kid on the New Jersey Owls. Coach Baccy Chew still remembers me as one of his more striking ball players.

But the most striking player on the Owls had to be ol' Gunky Gooch. Gunky would strike up a conversation with anybody. During the course of a season he struck out with more girls than any pitcher on the Jersey Owls. You could look it up.

Gunky was the kind of boy who struck fear into the hearts of parents with teenaged daughters. He was a slick talkin', greasy-haired, gangly southpaw who smoked a pack of Lucky Strike cigarettes per day.

Gunky fancied himself as bearing a striking resemblance to the rebel James Dean. Nowadays he'd be compared more to a character on "Laverne and Shirley." Coach Baccy Chew tolerated Gunky because the only thing slicker than his hairdo was his curve ball.

In 1961, the Owls faced the Katchell Kings in the State Tournament quarterfinals. The games were played at night in Katchell Memorial Park because Mr. Katchell liked to come home from the real estate office to watch his sons play ball.

The Katchells were monsters. All of them stood six feet tall, had black crew-cut hairdos, and absolutely no necks.

Matthew Katchell was a pitcher. Mark played first base, Luke played second, and Ruth Katchell would have been a pretty darn good shortstop if her daddy had let her.

We also figured Ruth was really supposed to be a boy named John, but that just shows ya how baseball can be a funny game...

Anyway, ol' Gunky hated the Katchells. When fate (plus identical 11-1 records) put us against them in the quarterfinals, Gunky wanted to beat 'em bad.

Through 8½ innings Gunky somehow kept them from scoring. He was pitching about the best we'd ever seen—and smoking about the worst. Gunk was so nervous by the time the bottom of the ninth rolled around, he'd smoked up all his Lucky Strikes.

Coach Chew knew Gunky had lost both his nerve and his curve, but our outfield was fast and the infield was lucky, so he left him in.

Dark rain clouds slowly covered the moon. Since our game was official after we'd played the seventh inning, the coach began praying for a cloudburst to end the inning. The entire team was counting on the rain caving in before Gunky did.

It was 1-0, our favor, as Gunky faced the final batter. Mr. Katchell came to the plate. Coach Chew called time and gave another glance skyward (rainward?) as he walked to the mound.

Before Chews reached him, Gunky took off his hat and baseball shoes. Then he started dancing. Dancing and hopping and bouncing on the pitcher's mound just like it was raining. The crowd went silent. Maybe the pressure had gotten to Gunky Gooch after all.

All of a sudden the brightest, loudest strike of lightning you ever saw came down from the sky. And it did start to rain. Pouring down rain. The umpires ruled the game was over.

Next day the paper read: "Final Score—Owls 1-Katchells 0" as Gunky's lightning strikes out the side. *—June 1981*

# Lady Barons showed up, showed spirited spunk

For five months, October through February, I coached 10 Elizabethtown Community College basketball players—ten crazy, shrewd, dumb, original, unpredictable, and unforgettable young women. Coach them? It took me most of the season to catch up with them…

Armed with my whistle and my intercollegiate basketball rulebook, blessed by my athletic director and by my young wife (the former's blessing coming somewhat easier than the latter's), I took over the team. Time would soon tell that these tools would not be enough.

The rulebook did explain the new 30-second shot clock, but not what to do about boyfriends meeting players during away games. I could look up an accurate description of a charging foul but nowhere did the book warn me of the charge Rod Stewart and Barry Manilow might give my young forwards, centers, and guards.

The whistle I wore did get their attention in October. But could it alone hold that attention through February? No chance, coach.

A community college basketball player treats her team as one of many activities vying for her time. She often juggles classes, school clubs, church work, homework, parents, parties, boyfriends, and Burger Queens at one time. (It seemed that half our team had a part-time job at Burger Queen.)

And believe me, our schedule demanded that I keep their attention. Our two-year college did not have the luxury or the equity of playing similarly-sized and skilled schools. As a ball team we had to go begging for games. This meant we often played the four-year institutions like Centre and Berea colleges and Transylvania University. Such schools got quality players by awarding athletic scholarships.

Our college did not award such scholarships. Since every team did (even the other two-year schools we played), I felt like my kids had to go up against pros—kids who got money to play ball. It seemed at times that an opponent ran up the score in order to justify their scholarship program. My players played ball only because they loved to.

Not surprisingly, our opponents loved to play us. I couldn't help but notice that we were always scheduled as a "Homecoming" or "President's Day" game when we traveled. I may have been a young coach but I knew what that meant. You see, an athletic director will usually try to schedule the local school of the blind for their homecoming game.

But we showed up for every game. We won a couple and even scared a homecoming queen or two. I may have enjoyed these away games most of all...on such trips I was van driver, meal moneyman, and coach—in that order.

My wife, who also works at the college, traveled with the team when she could. The players called her "Coachette." She could enter the sanctity of the locker room when I could not. She could overhear problems that as coach, I needed to know. And she could spot an unwanted boyfriend at 1,000 paces. Oftentimes I considered her the most valuable player of the road trip.

Home games were also fun—we played in the National Guard Armory. Our club dressed in either the old radio room or the kitchen. The radio shack was hot and cramped, about 6 by 12 feet. The kitchen was bright and cheery but the players didn't appreciate the tall, curtainless windows.

If a player got injured—boy was that girl in trouble. I was also the team trainer. I taped ankles, inspected jammed fingers and toes, cured the flu, and massaged egos…all the things my college degree in liberal arts had prepared me for.

I guess I knew when I took the job that we couldn't win many games. So maybe I coached for the beauty of it. I can tell you that it is a gift of beauty to work with 10 young people. They are all hope, promise, purpose, and pugnacity. I've heard other coaches say the kids help keep them young. I agree. Beauty, no matter what the form, is young. *—March 1981*

# DiMaggio's legend lives on

I am going to let you in on a secret. The New York City's sports world doesn't belong to a Ranger, or a Knick, Net, Met, Jet, or Giant. And it doesn't belong to any of the current New York Yankees. I lived back East for 21 years so I can tell you, the Big Apple belongs to one and only one sports figure, the great Joe DiMaggio.

How can I explain this to a Hardin County reader? Take Kyle Macy, Dan Issel, and mix them with the Fiddlin' Five and Rupp's Runts and toss in a nice Italian suit from Saint Rick and add Cawood's voice and then sing my Old Kentucky Home…and that's sort of the way New Yorkers feel about Jolting Joe DiMaggio.

Growing up in an Italian-American household, well, Joe D. was big. How big was he? Let me just say me and my brother were taught to count up to five, not to ten, because on our block the thinking was number five got you as close to God as one human could get.

DiMaggio's number was five.

These days you will run into a sports nut who'll trot out statistics proving Joe DiMaggio wasn't the greatest hitter in baseball. Such guys, if they lived in Hardin County, would probably actually like Bobby Knight and root for a Duke Blue Devil, whatever that is…

The point is, if you want to explain baseball to a Martian from outer space, I mean really show the green-eyed bugger baseball's glory and its grace, all you'd have to do is show him Joe DiMaggio rounding second base trying to stretch a double into something more.

I remember the stories in Sal's Italian-American barbershop where my brother and I got haircuts. Sal, the proprietor barber, held court. A short, portly but stately man, Sal was an artist with a comb and clippers. He didn't ask you how you wanted your hair cut, he already knew. He asked questions about how school was going.

"Hey Char-loots. (Sal calls me this to this very day.) Charloots, how's you do on Miss Benni's spelling test? Paul Picone was in today and he say he beat you by four words. I'm gonna a-tell your Momma when I see her come shopping down the street. What's the matter for you? You no study? How can you spell if you no study? If you come to my shop, you spell the best or you sweep the floor before I cut your hair.

Sal mixed his own hair tonics and was said to grind his own talc powder. He'd been president of the Chamber of Commerce twice. Our church's new basketball floor got installed because one August Sal donated his entire month's earnings. And August was his busiest month because all the kids got their back-to-school haircuts. Sal was the glue to our community.

Sal carried the Sporting News and the New York Times as well as the Daily News and Time Magazine in his barbershop. We'd wait for our haircuts and read about the world and about sports, the greatest of which was baseball. And the greatest player was the Yankee Clipper, the 56-game hitting streak hero, Jolting Joe DiMaggio.

Sal showed my brother and me how to sit up straight and how to look the world right in its eye. He cut hair but preached a local neighborhood gospel that said be proud to be an American first, and an American with Italian blood second. And, after you honored your parents and listened to the Priest you looked to one man as an example—to the great DiMaggio, the hope, the grace, the number five in Yankee pinstripes.

Once, some guy stopped in for a quick trim. Upon seeing DiMaggio's photo on Sal's mirror and reading its inscription, "To Sal, the true Yankee Clipper. Your pal, Joe D" the yahoo said,

"Ah DiMaggio was okay, but he was overrated. Ted Williams was a better ballplayer and the better man."

Well, Sal didn't say a word. He trimmed, clipped, and held his tongue. Then the joker asked for a hot shave. My brother and I winced as Sal stroked his straight razor to a cruel sharp edge. Sal's hands were thick and strong. We figured snapping this joker's neck would save Sal from ruining a good razor…

But Sal kept cool. Sal was courteous and professional. He clipped him, gave him talc, and walked with the man to the cash register. He rang up "No Sale" and as the man gave a puzzled look, Sal said, "You go now. I no take-a your money and you no ever come back. Next time you need a shave you ask it from Mr. Ted William's."

"But Sal," my brother asked, "why didn't you take that guy's money? You cut his hair."

"No, my little sir, no. When I cut his hair I didn't care. I cut but I no cared. To take money under such a circumstance would be a lie. When the great Joe DiMaggio play, they ask him, Joe why do you always play so hard? When the game is in the late innings and your team so far ahead, why you not take it easy? And do you know what Joe say?"

The entire barbershop paused. Benny, the man in the dark suit who always read the racing page, looked up over his paper. Old Mr. Carizzi, who sat by the radio tuning and re-tuning it to WPIX for the Yankee game, he shut the set entirely off. The two old-timers drinking espresso and playing chess paused and palmed their cigarettes between thumb and index finger like all the old timers from the old country did. My brother and I held our breath, as Sal explained,

"Joe say he always played hard and played his best because somebody might be watching him from high in the stands for the first time. There was only one way to be Joe DiMaggio, and that was your very best. Every play, be your best. For those people who might be seeing him for the first time, he played his best. You hear me boys. Spelling test? Then you spell your best. Sweep the sidewalk? You sweep your best. Kabish? When I cut hair and no put in my heart, then I dishonor the great Mr. DiMaggio and myself. So, that customer can go because he doesn't know what my heart knows. Good riddance to him."

The world in 1999 is a different place I guess. Today's athletes claim not to be role models. I don't know. The whole darn world could stand a long look in Sal's barbershop mirror if you ask me…

Anyhow, last weekend they reported Joe DiMaggio died. Then they said the report was in error. As I write this I have a feeling Joe is hanging in there but after rounding second base his legs feel a bit heavy. Maybe the next bag looks pretty far away. My heart goes out to him. I hope he gets to feeling better. No, I hope he gets to feeling like the best. *—January 1999*

# To dream when you are young

The phone rang late Tuesday night. I was half-asleep and dreaming. The caller didn't say hello, she asked, "Is it really you?" I yawned and said, "I certainly am really me, who wants to know?"

She was Diane, my cheerleader in 1971 at Ramapo High. She used to rah and ray my name. Mostly she called this during high school basketball games. Yes, I recognized Diane's voice. I could never forget her voice.

Truth is, I always felt sorry for her. Since my last name wasn't crisp and snappy she used to struggle with her cheer: "Rah-S Ray-P Rah-A Ray-T Rah-A Ray-R and O, Rah-Ray Chuck Spataro!" Poor Diane. My name took half the game to spell out. And I still only shot 69 percent from the free-throw line.

Today's call came from the Louisville airport. Diane was flying through town, an architect now, building mansions up and down the eastern seaboard. To kill time during a two-hour layover in Louisville she'd befriended a genuine Kentucky gentleman. This local had given Diane his copy of the "Hardin County Independent" because she told him how she loved reading small town weeklies when she traveled around the country on business.

That's how Dee came to find my familiar toothy grin staring out at her. So she called information and tracked me down. Small world, huh?

Back in a younger, even smaller world at Ramapo High Diane and I were keen on each other. We used to dream about settling down in a small town. The romance of someday moving to a good town in a place like Kentucky kept us together for most of our senior year. Such dreamers we were.

The dream was to buy a "small" but elegant plantation. I'd wear white suits and grow Colonel Sanders' beard. Dee would dress in ball gowns. We'd race horses and raise children. In my spare time I'd write the Great American Novel while Dee would decorate our house like the set of "Gone With The Wind."

It was the kind of bubble-mush high school seniors used to blow into tall glasses of ice cream sodas on Friday nights. We dreamt it after every home game, win or lose.

I rubbed some sleep from my eyes as we exchanged our "how-are-you's" and the "it's-been-years." Diane said she was almost afraid to call. She wasn't sure I'd be me.

"I didn't recognize your picture on the column. But that crazy name was familiar. I'll never forget how to spell S-p-a-t-a-r-o."

I guess not. Some things we chant to ourselves in high school have a way of sticking. Like chewing gum.

"It was your beard that threw me," she continued, "Coach barely allowed you guys to have hair on your heads, now you've grown it all over your face."

"The beard," I explained, "hides my foolish youth and covers all the missed free throws. It is not exactly a Colonel Sanders' special, but it was the best I could do. Anyway, I only put it on when I go out."

"Yes," Diane said, "it is you. A little funny, a bit incoherent, and you still can't shoot or talk straight to save your life."

So I asked her if she still wore the tightest uniform on her team. She said her firm was loaded with former high school dream-queens, so nobody even noticed her anymore. I laughed. She waited a long while and then she laughed too.

"Dee, it's good to hear your voice," I said.

"Chuck, it's good to see your smile. A bit hairier, but still the same dreamer's smile."

She asked if I had written any novels. I told her I wrote columns. I asked if she'd found that plantation and she said no, but she and her husband named their first daughter, Tara.

"I guess we were young back then," she said, "and silly dreamers. A famous writer and the high society queen. Dreams."

"Dreams," I agreed. "But you're supposed to dream when you are young." — *February 2001*

*Chapter Five*

# Cove Columns

# Falling stars sing

I saw a falling star last night. We have a dock down by the cove especially built for watching stars fall. Some people prefer to call them Shooting Stars and others say meteorites—but falling stars seems most correct if not quite as precise.

Once or twice a week in summer I get someone, a neighbor kid, a dinner guest, or my Mrs. to keep me company down by this dock. And we count the stars, fall. When the moon reflects off the water just right, it looks like these falling stars are diving straight into a pool of moon-made light, heading light to light and fire to fire.

I know this Astronomy Professor at the University of Kentucky who says meteors make a singing sound as they fall. This is sort of a controversial topic among astronomers, so I'm told. In fact, most scientists doubted this "singing effect" could be physically produced by a burning/gaseous rock lunging through earth's atmosphere.

But this UK professor took a team of grad school scholars up to the coldest Russia Siberian plain and they stayed up late watching the sky until they managed to get a tape recording of a meteor as it fell. It was a major scientific find. A real career booster for any professor. They wrote up a scholarly paper and even put the tape on the Internet so anybody could listen to a falling star.

I managed to get my Harmony Cove computer (read: Mrs. Spataro figured out how to work Real Audio) hooked up and listened. It sounded like a big static CRACKLE and POP. Sort of disappointing to tell you the truth. I was just wondering if the good Professor's assistant might have gotten too close to the microphone with his breakfast cereal?

Seems like they went to a lot of trouble, traveling way up there in coldest Russia, camping out in skimpy tents with microphones and all sort of scientific gear when they could have come to our dock. We listen to falling stars all the time around here. In fact, we discovered singing songs attracts shooting stars.

Whenever I get some Harmony Cove kids to join us on the falling star dock we always sing the stars down. I ask the kids to sing (softly now, because you don't want to scare them off), humming tunes like "*twinkle, twinkle little star*..."

And with older neighborhood kids I bring my ancient cassette tapes along (Hey Mr. S. we didn't know they had recorded music back when you were young?) and play stuff like Sly Stone's "Everybody is a star."

On tough, hard-to-find-a-star nights, I use special diversionary tactics. I bring lots of Ding Dongs and Ho-Ho chocolate cakes wrapped in silver foil. After stuffing the chocolate in our mouths we lay back and toss the tin foils up skyward, hoping a star will notice the sparkle and dive down for a looky-see.

Many a clear summer's night the Mrs. and me have spent tucked inside a sleeping bag looking skyward. The ducks must think us a sight with our Coleman lantern glowing and a pile of Ding-Dong silver foils dotting the dock's old wooden planks like stars.

On my birthday's eve we always spend the night on the dock eating chocolate and making tin foils stars while we count falling stars. On good summer nights I've counted as many stars as years I've lived. This past June I counted 47 stars falling. But I can't be precise. Sometimes we laugh so hard the chocolate and the tears spoil our count.

I can testify for a fact I have heard the falling stars sing. They don't sound a thing like the professor's snap, crackle, and pop. But perhaps stars sound different to each individual...once again I defer to Mr. Sly Stone...different strokes for different folks. Mrs. Spataro swears she hears Jiminy Cricket calling, "*When you wish upon a star...*" but most nights I hear Perry Como's "*Catch a falling star and put it in your pocket, save it for rainy day.*" *—July 2000*

# Cove's magic delivered in 30 dreams or less

I've been around Hardin County this past week attending a reception for the new president at ECC (and other public functions where there was free food) and several people have stopped me to ask, "Where's Harmony Cove and what's it like to live there?"

Where and what indeed.

This column is a road map to Harmony Cove, Ky. In my own style, all I am trying to get you to do is come visit me, come sit with me on the rose-backed bench beside the water and watch as the fireflies dance across the cove's rock-lined edge. I invite you to sip a glass of sun tea with me as I try to explain to my "Big Blue" next-door neighbor why college basketball shouldn't have a shot clock. And between stories about the time my editor Gerald Lush once rang the Liberty Bell and around my lies concerning why

Hemmingway's short stories are greater art than his novels, I hope we share our reflection in the cove, maybe for just an instant.

But if you really want to get to know Harmony Cove well, here's what I understand about the place.

First you need to realize it is a real place here in Hardin County. It's a place where the grass carp grow to the size of "Maybe Dick" and the catfish growl at night. Harmony Cove is part of a small lake fed by more than 40 freshwater springs. I would have called the lake "40 Springs Lake" had I been there when they named it, but I wasn't. Or, I might have called it Dogwood Lake because of the white glorious dogwoods surrounding the water. Maybe I would have called it Reflection Lake had I been there when the good ol' boys got to picking names, but I wasn't there. I was still looking for it.

The lake is a place where 40 or so houses ring the water, houses that range from quiet log cabins to rusting old fishermen's trailers. We claim a mix of fishermen, prominent citizens, possible criminals, and a bearded, bald-headed poet or two among our membership. Every Fourth of July there's a cookout when we each say hello, but mostly it's a quiet place.

Harmony Cove is where I live. It is unique because unlike the other places on the lake, Harmony Cove rests directly beneath the exact center of the Milky Way galaxy. It says so on the deed to my house. (If that realtor ever moves back to Hardin County, I've got to ask him how he figured it.)

Looking up at the stars at night I often see the constellation Cassiopeia and her outstretched arms straddling her hush of stars. Now and then she waves from her throne on the Milky Way and I wave back without a word.

I often wonder what sounds she hears up in the heavens. At the cove I hear the gentle drift of lake water over the boat dock piles. I listen to the wings of geese and wind and the far off clanging of our clubhouse's flagpole. When the lifeguards at the pool don't tie the flagpole cord up tight, it strikes the silver pole ringing like a church bell. (On days when the guards do remember to tie the cord tight, I usually slip down to the pool around midnight and loosen the knots just enough to hear the bell ring.)

I suspect Cassiopeia up in her Milky Way heaven hears much the same sounds, for stardust can't sound much different than geese feathers, bell rings, and earth wind.

Harmony Cove itself is about 50 yards long and shaped like a liquid crescent moon. She's (I'm quite certain she's a she) mostly green and usually full of grass carp and turtles. Mrs. Spataro would tell you how the cove is also full of my reading glasses that I've spilled into the water from our boat the Jolly Rogers. Rogers is the name the Mrs. went by before all my poetry and peculiarity turned her to matrimony. She says it was like Darth Vader being turned to the dark side, but I think she's joking.

My copy of Whitman's "Leaves of Grass" is also down in that cove. It was the first book I dropped into the water. It happened quite by accident as I was crossing the bridge that connects Harmony Cove to the island in its center, and I thought I saw a Civil War saber in the water. I leaned over the bridge to get a better look; the book popped from my back pocket into the cove. A grass carp gobbled it up in one gulp.

Now once a year, on my birthday in fact, I drop another book of poetry into the cove. I believe a good cove must be restocked (just like they restock fish) with magic, and I've found the poetry of Whitman and the prose of Abraham Lincoln works very well here in Kentucky.

Maybe you want to come visit Harmony Cove? Better yet, you could build a cove of your own. I have sort of a side business where I come to lakes and coves across Kentucky and provide a starter stock of magic. If you've got the place, call me and I'll bring some of the magic. Cost? Fifty cents at the newsstand and we'll guarantee it for around a week. Just drop one in your pool.

*— June 1998*

# Come to the cove for a whirlwind tour

You'd like the loft here at Harmony Cove. It is the place I come to write. Before I bought Harmony Cove the loft was used by a local E-town artist who had her easel and oils set up there. I love the natural light (both sun and moonlight) as it streams through the windows.

The sunbeams and moonbeams bounce across the tomb for the unknown junk mail (as Mrs. S. calls my desk), ricochet off some bookcases, and touch my life-sized poster of the godfather of Hardin County radio, Mr. Ron Boone. Mrs. Spataro has a corner up here too, where she pays the bills, balances the checkbook, and somehow manages to keep me out of jail. Well, so far...

You get to the loft by climbing a winding spiral staircase. Heading up to write these columns I feel like a bent-backed, gray-bearded, lighthouse keeper climbing a tower. Climbing to shine the lamp on Hardin County. Upstairs the loft's long glass windows face south and west. Like a lighthouse keeper scanning the sea, I can see most of Hardin County from up top the loft. Especially late at night when the dark skies are clear. Then you feel like you can almost reach out and touch the county's courthouse steps...

Maybe a scientist should come and study the freak optics and visual illusions disseminating from high atop Harmony Cove.

Scientists? Nahh...what do they know of cool, starry nights and how clear the constellations sparkle green in the cove water? How could a scientist measure the peace and beauty of our heartland? No, not scientists...you come with me.

You come. It's late, just past midnight, but you come with me. Come climb the spiral steps and look as together we see our hearts in Hardin County beating in the quiet night. It's late, but climb and come look with me...

There's a nurse at Hardin Memorial Hospital. She is standing at the window on the third floor. She's worried tonight. A passing car's headlight catches her Elizabethtown Community College nursing pin and it sparkles green like a star. Must be a little one who's not doing well. I have seen this nurse watch from her window many nights before. The hospital must be a good place. If their nurses worry enough to go to the window and say a little prayer, well, I guess you can't find a better nurse than that. Take care young nurse. We are all a part of your prayer tonight.

There's a police cruiser pulling out of Wal-Mart's parking lot. He has a bag of fresh donuts in one hand and a list of boys in the other. It's a baseball team. He'll be doing some volunteer work with Big Brothers/Big Sisters tomorrow on his day off. So how are you going to juggle that starting line-up, Coach? One boy's dad only comes home to beat up his mom. How will you teach this boy patience and to wait on a curve ball?

These good officers in Hardin County really never have a day off. They do their jobs, mostly long, boring routine days but then come those moments of cut-glass courage: the drug busts, the violent family quarrels, the tragic auto accidents. We are lucky for such good men and women. Peacekeepers. I'd gladly share the price of that donut bag with you my friend. You deserve so much more than our mere thanks.

Look over there at ECC. That new faculty member is still at his desk. With summer school already in session and the fall's freshmen due in for orientation, he's got plenty to do. It's a good place, that tiny college. Good because of folks like Dr. Jim Owen and Dr. George Luster and Mr. Robert Keen, folks who built the college nearly forty years ago. Built the place with a few bricks, mortar, and piles of integrity. A group called the North Central Kentucky Education Foundation can tell you all about integrity and these men. Wait, the young professor's just shut his light off. Calling it a night...but he'll back in the office in six hours...sleep well.

Look now across town, a candle glows in St. James Catholic Church. A member of the parish has slipped inside to pray. Now she lights a candle. She knows of a sick baby at the hospital. She lights two candles, one for the child and one for, well, one just because. The priest, unable to sleep, comes into the church. Father has been comforting a nurse at the hospital. In the church Father and parish member smile to one another, but ask no questions, share no words. It is almost 2 a.m. This sacred place holds just these two souls but seems full, seems somehow bursting with candlelight and hope.

Somehow...hope? We are lucky in Hardin County. We have so many rich hearts filling the pews of so many fine churches and places of worship. "Why do these children suffer so?" the young nurse had asked Father an hour ago. Then the priest had said nothing. He only stared at the teary-eyed nurse and watched as she lit a cigarette. Now, striking a match to a candle, a calm smile forms on his face as he says, "Lamb of God who takes away the sins of the world, have mercy on us..."

By the courthouse a jogger is circling the old building. The bank's clock down the road says 2:22 a.m. Isn't it strange for a jogger to be up and about this late? Why so restless, why so late? Restless most nights, the man jogs. He was phased out of a life-long job on post two months ago. So now, restless at night he jogs. Each step is a job-wanted ad crossed out. He's pushing, planning, thinking out his next job interview. Maybe as he passes the Small Business Development Center office downtown he will think about starting that clock repair shop. It's just a dream. But many a dream's come true in Hardin County. There are clocks all across Hardin County ticking but not running on time. Maybe a good man with a good steady hand is needed, a gentle adjustment perhaps. A light in the dark to show the way...

What's this light in a garage down near Glendale? Who could be fixing a bicycle this late at night? It's a young mother, whose arms ache from her factory day job. School's out and her child needs a safe bike to fly the summer by... And Mom knows her alarm clock for work will ring in just four hours. But she doesn't care. She is fixing her daughter's bike while still ringing sweetly in her ears is how her child asked, "Pretty please, Mommy" as she tucked the little one into bed. The new bike is a 10-speed, a neon green beauty. One less speed than I need, thinks mom...

There goes the late freight train North towards E'town. Many, many bikes, some neon green, some not, hang in the bicycle shop's display window across from Pritchard Community Center. With the train's passing, bicycles sway like church bells swinging.

Into the bike shop's parking lot pulls the police officer with his empty donut bag and baseball roster. Just a routine check on the bike shop's lock and then he can head home. All clear, all safe, and secure. All locked up for the night. Meanwhile back at the police station a nearly cold cup of coffee trembles on the dispatcher's desk as the train slowly passes by...

I can just barely hear the train's whistle here at Harmony Cove. But from the loft I can clearly see how the coffee ripples on the dispatcher's desk. I see the Hardin Memorial Hospital nurse standing at the windowsill, her pin glimmering like a signal fire. And a desk lamp still glows out at ECC, while at St. James Church a candle flickers steady and low, a hymnal glow.

I can see them all, love them all, and with my heart to each and every one call. I can see clearly how a child's handlebar bell trembles in the grace of Hardin County's green night, her good, green night. I'm glad you all could come tonight. Good night.
*— June 1998*

# Cove cocoa's magic warms the soul

Ah, the fall. The cool days and crisp nights. The season for warm mugs full of hot drinks. Coffees? Teas? Please, not for me. What I long for in autumn is a cup of Edina and Emma's Harmony Cove Cocoa.

Sisters Edina and Emma Wells have been making their precious cocoa mix since 1953. In fact, the chocolate-colored tins each come with "Harmony Cove 1953" inscribed upon the label.

The tins do not even say cocoa but there's no mistaking what's inside as soon as you pop open the lid. The world has never smelled a more luxurious, heaven-inspired powder for mixing heart-warming hot chocolate.

Food critics from across the state have tried to decipher its secret ingredients. Some say the cocoa has a genuine old time flavor.

The Wells sisters do all the work by hand. In the last few years demand for Harmony Cove 1953 cocoa mix has grown phenomenally. To match supply with demand the sisters have had to install a second wood stove to their log cabin here at the lake. And twice a week ol' Bobby Rose Combs, the ex-major league baseball grounds-keeper, cuts and delivers a load of hickory and ash.

"When we were younger," says Edina Wells, "Emma and I really did it all. I carried the water up from the cove while Emma chopped and split the logs for the wood stove. But mercy, we can't do that anymore. My eyes are just about gone and Emma does have a bit of a heart problem. The doctor says if Emma expects to live another sixty-five years she had better let Bobby Rose cut the wood."

"My heart indeed," says the bright-eyed Emma Wells. "I notice Dr. Sapsucker has increased his order from two tins to five this year, sister."

"I noticed that as well, sister. You don't suppose he knows something we don't?"

"I believe you're making a joke at the expense of my good-hearted nature, sister."

"Well sister, your heart was my concern to be sure…"

Bobby Rose told me he gets ten "Harmony Cove 1953" tins for his labor. And if he could, he'd chop down a forest for a few more containers of the sisters' precious powder.

"I try to make my ten tins last the whole winter long, but there's no cocoa like the sister Wells' cocoa. I reckon my ten is the most any folks ever get in the whole world. But by New Year's

Eve I'm drinking a Kroger microwave chocolate mix like everyone else. I sure wish those ladies would sell me the recipe..."

But they won't. The secret recipe is something Edina and Emma just laugh about when asked. I asked them just last year and had my leg pulled until it hurt...

"Our SECRET recipe. Did you hear that Emma dear? This nice young man wants to know our secret. Do you remember our secret dear?"

"Why no, Edina. I thought you remembered. I forgot years ago. Don't you remember me telling you how I forgot? Oh dear. MAYBE YOUR MEMORY IS GOING TOO? If your memory goes, what will we do?"

And the two quick-witted women broke into peals of laughter.

"Here now. We were being rude. We apologize. But for more than forty years, fancy chefs, cooks, and big cocoa company crooks have been trying to steal our secret away. We don't mean to laugh at you. Here. Take this tin of cocoa mix back to that nice wife of yours. Tell her she is always welcome at the Wells' cabin. Good day Mr. Spataro."

Since my wife doesn't drink tea or coffee she's become a discerning critic of cocoa. When Joella tasted the "Harmony Cove 1953" mixture she couldn't believe how rich and chocolaty the stuff was. So she wrote Edina and Emma a little thank you and we have been getting one tin of "Harmony Cove 1953" every fall ever since.

So how do you get a tin of "Harmony Cove 1953?" If you have to ask, you probably are out of luck. The Wells sisters don't advertise and don't accept money or donations. I did ask them about how many tins they produced a year. Emma thinks it's two hundred. Edina will only say it's "probably more than the numbers of hairs left in that bald old columnist head of yours..."

That's Edina for you. You just don't want to get in her line of fire...Which is why I was so surprised when she came knocking at my door this weekend.

"Oh pardon this intrusion Mr. Spataro. Is your wife at home?"

"Hello Edina. No, Mrs. Spataro is shopping. Can I tell her you stopped by?"

"Would you? And would you please say how sorry I was to have missed her. Maybe your wife could visit us sometime. I guess you heard Emma has been feeling poorly, and I think she'd like to meet the woman who wrote us such a nice thank you note about our cocoa."

Later my wife did visit the Wells sisters. Seems like they are making some changes. Because of Emma's health they're moving from the lake and heading south for a warmer climate. My wife said where they were going there wouldn't be much need for hot cocoa.

"The Wells sisters are leaving? Gosh, that's too bad. They broke the mold after those two were made. So why else did Edina want you to visit?"

"Oh she wanted to give me something."

"Something?"

"Yes, just something. Tell me Charles, would you mind cutting some extra firewood this fall. I'm going to need lots of firewood."

"You are?"

"Yes. And do you know that spring down by the east end of the lake?"

"You mean the natural spring flowing out of the old cave where they found the civil war campsite back in 1953? What about it?"

"Well, I'm going to need your help...There's something we need to get..." *— October 1998*

# Cove heron watches all

They say there's a Blue Heron at Harmony Cove who's more than 100 years old. I don't know. Creatures of flight are

magical enough to me without legends of timelessness. But I can testify to one great blue bird, gray and lingering near the shoreline, who just might be the "Big Blue" the old-timers dream about.

Clear summer mornings, when the new sun catches a few cloud puffs and cracks them soft pink like a breakfast egg, are when you'll see Big Blue. She's more gray than blue these days. What I wouldn't give to have a human conversation with her.

This morning she was across the lake near the nude beach. We have one spot where ol' Mr. Webster Buff was fishin' when he fell out of his boat. We saw him wade out of the lake towing his boat behind. But he'd lost his pants. Apparently Mr. Buff had "gone commando" that day because he wasn't wearing any bottoms. Not to miss a good morning's catch Webster just sat on a rock and finished playing the bass he'd snagged before wrapping himself (the bass too, come to think of it) in a green garbage bag and heading home.

We have since called that particular spot "the nude beach." It is also a favorite sitting spot for the Heron. Big Blue rests on the exact rock Webster Buff used to land his bass. Now I wonder what Big Blue thinks about sitting there on ol' Webster Buff's nude beach?

One thing I have noticed about Big Blue is that she never remains on the ground when a plane flies across Harmony Cove. With the E'town airport so close, we get plenty of private planes circling the lake; maybe they are looking for Webster to "show" himself or maybe they are attracted to the lake the way a bird will rush a glass window charging its own reflection. I don't know.

But I do know Big Blue takes to flight whenever a plane invades her airspace.

Does Blue think she can ward off the noisy mechanical impostors? Or is the Heron curious, seeking to know better the wings and beak of the Piper Cubs and Cessna's. I imagine Big Blue remembers the first time a prop-driven plane cut across the cove. Maybe then she flew directly towards it, defending her home. Now nearly a century later she is the champion of many jousts. Still a warrior bird but rather amazed at her continued success, old as she is. Her vision more a Monet-like mist than the sharp scope-eye of youth.

What does she think when charging higher and higher, lungs burning, passing the soft egg-crack pink of a morning cloud? Is this the last flight up? Will the mechanical bill and the metal wings finally triumph? Am I to fall helplessly only to drown in my own reflection?

Or is it still her cove, her time, her gift and right to rule the sky?

Oh, I guess I can't really believe Big Blue is 100 years old. But if she was, she'd be a contemporary of Wilbur and Orville Wright. It wasn't but 90 years ago in Kitty Hawk the Wrights took man's first leap in space. This historical fact is often pointed out to us at Harmony Cove by sweet old Ronnie Gibson. Ms. Gibson, a blue-haired spinster down at the southern end of our lake, says she remembers the Wright Brothers.

Well, she would. Ms. Gibson is sort of a character. She wears sandals year round and is rumored to spend an occasional night with Mr. Buff. She smiles and says they like 'going fishin' together now and then. Spinster Gibson says her father worked at a fire station near Kitty Hawk, North Carolina. Says the Wright Brothers hired her daddy and the other firemen to carry their flying machine across the sand dunes. People around Kitty Hawk thought the Wright brothers were crazy people.

Old Ms. Gibson says the Wright's were a dark-dressed duo who always wore thick, round-toed shoes on the beach. Says her daddy called them the "Bowler Brothers" because of the funny

"Bowler" hats they wore. Busy as bees they were too. Talked about their machine day and night, and nothing else. Ms. Gibson says she used to cover Orville's black boots with sand while he gave instructions to her father on how to aim the flying contraption's wings into the wind.

Well I never thought much about Ms. Gibson and her stories until the other day. I figured her being on up in years had jumbled her memory. Mrs. Spataro says I'm the same way now, and I'm only half her age...

But this past weekend I was up in the old clubhouse attic at the north side of the lake. There was a wedding party coming to use the clubhouse, and they wanted to know if we had any candleholders to lend for the ceremony. Spinster Gibson told me to look up in the clubhouse attic 'cause she remembered candlesticks and mementos tucked back there.

Sure enough I found the candleholders next to an old pile of newspapers. At first I thought they were some of Gerald Lush's early editions (but even Gerald isn't that old...). I thumbed through the stack until I saw the headline about a family just moved into town. Seems they were from the East Coast. The father worked in a fire station near the Carolina coast. His wife and second baby died shortly after childbirth and Mr. Gibson had moved to Kentucky with his only child.

In a section called "Hardin County Welcomes You" was a picture of Carl Gibson and his little daughter, a big blue-eyed girl in sandals. She was holding tight to the baby Heron brought with her from the ocean... *—July 2000*

# Sip a cove cocktail...it's the 'real thing'

While the county re-examines its wet/dry issue, here is the perfect drink for summer.

The Harmony Cove Cocktail isn't for everyone. But on long, slow, hot summer nights it's sweet and cool and quenching.

Like the Japanese Tea Ceremony, this Cove Cocktail is part ritual, part companionship, and part drink. For your pleasure I freely share this recipe.

Take one hot summer night, humid and still, the kind of night all summers become. Add a still moon, hot as neon, hanging above a dark green cove. Blend the stillness, the moon, and the midnight until all you can see, all you can feel, all you can know is summer-now, this evening, this moment tonight.

Find an old stereo, not some antiseptic compact disk player (CD's belong in banks). No, go search deep in your basement for an old turntable and your worn, scratchy 45-rpm records. You remember the black "dishes" you danced to when love was neon and hanging above a dark green cove.

Play an old tune, scratchy and low, perhaps Frankie Valli singing, "*You're just too good to be true, can't take my eyes off you.*" Take your best sweetheart in your arms holding each other close as Frankie sings, "*You'd be like heaven to touch, I want to hold you so much.*"

Dig out your old high school literature book and read a long forgotten love poem. Read it aloud. Remember when the poetry filled your heart; remember before the mortgages, before the car payments, before time broke its stillness and the moon was yet neon, a promise hanging above a dark green cove.

Now take two thick, old style milkshake glasses, the kind J.J. Newberry's had years ago when you grabbed a milkshake after just leaving the State Theater. Two thick glasses, the kind you cupped tenderly with your sweetheart recalling the screams from "Jaws," and how you blew bubbles through your straw to the tune of the shark's theme...daa-da, daa-da, dadadadadada.

Or recalling the ill-fated lovers in "Love Story," and how love meant never saying you're sorry. Maybe your Newberry's milkshake came after Butch Cassidy and the Sundance Kid had died leaving Katherine Ross's big round eyes full of tears. Recalling a summer faded from the silver screen.

Now fill a blender with rich vanilla ice cream. Add two bottles (not cans, not those silly plastic boxes) of Yoo Hoo chocolate drink. Take ten—no, better make that fourteen—chocolate chip cookies and crush them into the blender. Add two long, hard squeezes of rich maple pancake syrup. Squeeze a third round and press the blender button labeled "smooth."

Pour the Cove Cocktail into your chilled, heavy shake glasses. Add two plump cherries and you're almost ready. But first set the stereo to repeat and repeat the same scratchy old 45.

Open the windows so the thick, humid summer's air and the cool neon moon drift in allowing the music to slip out, taking its place outside.

With one hand holding tight to your baby and the other squeezing the Cove Cocktail, you dance. "*You'd be like heaven to touch, I want to hold you so much. Trust in me when I say...*"

You dance slowly, barefoot in the summer night. You dance with the hot, humid summer night. On the coffee table near the TV (dead as it should be) rests a Scrabble game and candles lit. But now you dance. The dance is slow; perhaps your bare foot touches the letter "y" and brushes the letter "u." But you dance. The record plays. The moon is round and shiny like vinyl. Perhaps the scratchy 45 will play until dawn. Perhaps, the thick, cold Harmony Cove Cocktail, if sipped slowly, will last until dawn as well. Perhaps the moon and the ice cream will be all the nourishment you'll need the long summer through.

"*I love you baby and if it's quite all right, I need you baby to warm a lonely night. Oh pretty baby, trust in me when I say...*"
*—July 1998*

# Cove Cloudship nearing takeoff

Well, it's Sunday night but I finally got the Harmony Cove hot air balloon airworthy. I've been using some old nylon band flags donated by high schools from around the Heartland, sewing each colorful flag into the bulb-shaped belly of my balloon.

It was slow work. My old foot-pedal-driven sewing machine didn't help speed the work. Neither did the time my cat jumped up onto the sewing table catching his tail in the bobbin. This was practically a sequel to the mean old Mr. Grinch cartoon as I sat sewing my balloon to my cat's chagrin.

Jumper's fine, our vet says most of his tail fur should grow back by Christmas.

I'd like to apologize to the Heartland Committee for missing the balloon glow, and for missing the Buck Chase. My next-door neighbors went to the balloon glow and said it was stunning. Especially the yellow Kroger balloon and how the fire filled the yellow balloon canvass like a Japanese lantern lighting a pool party on prom night. I heard that the "Just for Kids" hospital balloon tipped slightly during its balloon glow inflation and brushed gently against a neighboring airship. One kid turned to his mom and said, "Look, the balloons are kissing…"

Kids love hot air balloons. I think it goes back to the Judy Garland movie, "The Wizard of Oz." This film has become America's bedtime story. The one fairy tale we are all told (through the magic of television) and all believe as we believe nothing else. Even as adults, who among us hasn't looked about his surroundings and thought, "I don't think we're in Kansas anymore?"

Remember the film? How the black and white reality burst into the Technicolor of Oz? Remember the scary witches, flying monkey monsters, and talking trees? And for children it is often their very first encounter with a hot air balloon.

As adults we still can recall how the wicked witch melted, how the monkey monsters scared the bejesus out of us, and, how a hot air balloon took the wizard home but left Dorothy stranded. If you're like me, hot air balloons have held you in their clutches from Dorothy's adventure on until today. They tease our collective conscious with their grace and optimism yet frighten us because of their unpredictability. Their images carry the promise of flight, escape, and perhaps freedom (somewhere over the rainbow?) but as Dorothy discovers, you can't guarantee where they'll go, or when.

This fascination with balloons pursues us even in this age of supersonic jets. One rich adventurer or another seems always to be launching some high-tech balloon for a solo flight around the world only to crash in somc cold sea. And crowds never fail to turn out to see balloons glow at Derby Week festivals or some similar public party.

I understand the allure. There is something lovely about a hot air balloon. Even carrying the commercial messages they often do, there is still an innocence about them. My own cove air craft is proof of the power of the balloon upon an otherwise reasonable (huh?) man's mind.

This homemade balloon of mine is a beauty, though. Once I got all the band flags sewn together I dyed the whole thing a deep lake water green. Then I painted a silver catfish smiling a whiskery grin as he leaps over a fishing boat...

Saturday night came and the cloud ship still wasn't ready. I'd run out of silver paint for the fish so me and the Mrs. jumped into the car and drove to Target. This was about 9 p.m. Saturday night. Coming out of Target I kept hearing a booming sound. Sure enough there over the tree line were the fireworks from the Festival.

We sat in the parking lot with the other Target shoppers and watched the sky sparkle in spectacular Fourth of July-like colors. There is something delicious in not expecting to see the fireworks and then accidentally discovering their presence. We looked across a side road, up and over the garage where a line of silent Hardin County School buses lay sleeping. Their rows of glass windows blinked in reflection of the blues, reds, and indigo rockets crossing the star-dusk sky.

It was at the grand finale Mrs. Spataro bet me a "Reach for the Stars" Heartland T-shirt that I'd never get the Harmony Cove balloon made in time for Heartland 1998. Darn. She was right, as usual. But seeing the fireworks exploding above those gentle yellow school buses was quite a sight. Glad to have seen it. And if the cove cloud-ship hadn't been running behind schedule we'd have never been in that Target parking lot late Saturday night. So, something's lost but something's gained.

The Cove Cloud-ship is up and flying now. It is late Sunday night and all the Heartland events are over. I'm high above Freeman Lake surveying the scene. Even from way up here the Freeman Lake Park looks glorious and the bandstand seems huge. I can even see tread marks where an elegant white stretch limousine parked after escorting the "Association" to the stage.

I am a little bit worried about the wind tonight. I may need to finish writing this column soon and see if I can set the balloon down. Or maybe I'll try to pass over the spacious offices of the Independent there on North Mulberry and drop the column down the chimney. The wind is really kicking up…

Before I turn all my attention to piloting this air-ship (where did Joella say she put those instructions on flying a balloon?) I do want to say one more thing about the Heartland Festival. Many thanks to the community leaders who combined to bring the classic rock band "The Association" to our Heartland. My neighbors said it was a great concert, drawing standing ovations from a very appreciative crowd. This beloved sixties band sang such group hits as "Cherish" and "Along Came Mary." I hear the highlight of their show was an updated version of the old Left Bank tune "Walk Away Renee." Great sounds.

Come to think of it, maybe it is because of the Association that I'm having such trouble maneuvering this balloon…

Because whenever the Association comes to town, "*Everyone knows it's windy…*" *—September 1998*

# A dreary day buoyed by a yellow balloon

There is a girl, maybe seven years old, who passes by Harmony Cove on her way to the bus stop. Two toothpick legs in rain boots stick out beneath a pink raincoat. She walks very fast, and I have seen her skip and run a step or two as she passes by.

She passed today with a yellow balloon trailing her like a kite on a string. A bright, shining, yellow balloon. And as she passes she cranks her head around as if to check whether her yellow friend was enjoying the ride to school. And then they were gone.

I turned my attention to other chores, a leaky pipe in the basement, a report saying the most significant event of the 20th century was the atom bomb's explosion, and the Donnie and Marie morning show had on Ally McBeal. Same old stuff.

As the day drifted by, the plumber came and took away the leak, I decided the Beatles and not the atom bomb made a bigger sound in the past 99 years, and Donnie told Ally to please eat something before the next commercial break.

I read the paper about how President Clinton's approval ratings were higher than ever and how Monica Lewinsky had been nominated as the most important female in the news. CNN did a live remote from Mississippi where a judge was about to rule on whether or not the Ten Commandments had to be taken down from a third-grade classroom wall.

It was a warm, spring-like March morning. Wet, but clearing. And on National Public Radio down on the Western Kentucky University campus they had Tony Bennett singing, "*fly me to the moon and let me play amongst the stars, let me see what springtime's like on Jupiter and Mars.*" I was about to start in doing my taxes, the kitchen table buried in crumpled papers and torn receipt stubs. And as my second pencil point broke I couldn't agree more with Mr. Bennett's choice of location.

The cats caught a mouse, or a vole, to be more precise. I rescued the critter from two very perturbed great hunters (a vole is about as big and fierce as Donnie Osmond without the teeth) and set it free outside in the garden. Suddenly both cats had an irresistible urge to go gardening. But I am a wise reader of newspapers, listener to NRP radio, and watcher of CNN Live. Those cats didn't fool me.

I finished doing the taxes (read: I gave up and Joella will figure it out) and knocked out another scene on my soon-to-be-released novel. (The part where Pamela Sue Anderson calls me saying "Oh Chuck, you've got to come over and help me straighten out my thong.") It's a murder mystery novel. The mystery is how at my age I still remember what a thong is; the murder comes as soon as my wife reads it.

Then Tony Bennett finished singing. NPR radio did a report on the white supremacist in Texas who killed a black man by dragging him tied on a chain to the rear of a truck. The story drifted in and out or my ability to listen to such horror did. The accused killer passed incriminating notes to a cellmate while awaiting trial. These notes in prison jargon are called "kites." The notes were all but a complete and remorseless confession to his crime. I was struck by the image of the tortured man, dangling from the end of the logging chain, bleeding to death like a human kite.

Kites indeed.

At about two thirty I began picking up the house. I'm a normal house husband when it comes to clean-ups. I stuff my dirty clothes under the bed, hide the tax papers under the couch, and as for my bathroom, well, I just shut the door. The EPA guys come over every first Monday of the month and do that chore.

What a day. The atom bomb and the plumber came. Two ferocious cats attacked a vole, while Clinton and Lewinsky continued dancing on CNN. I was thinking about flying a kite and then, couldn't. The Tony Bennett music was touching, and so was how Donnie hugged his sister Marie after the show. It was a calm, rainy March day mixed with ordinary horror stories, made more real by their ordinariness. My thoughts have come out a jumble, puréed by the media. And maybe the best I can say is there but for the grace of God go I.

Somehow, what mattered most was the yellow balloon. *— March 1999*

# Mallard's cruel fate—life's lesson

I buried a beautiful mallard duck this morning.

I've watched some young drivers near our lake play a game where they speed up their cars as the ducks scatter from the road. Most of the time the cars just barely miss the birds. When the weather is warm and the car windows are down I can hear stereos booming and the boys (Why is it always boys, never girls?) laughing as they play this deadly game of chicken with the ducks.

People tell me boys will be boys. And I know there are worse things these days to worry over, namely Kosovo and all the inhumane evils going on over there. And I believe most of our local teens are good kids, maybe a bit angry, maybe a little out of focus, but basically good underneath it all.

Most times the mallard gets away. Most times I hear a horn blow and the sound of wings scattering. Then comes a splash safely in the water. But every now and then a bird is lame, or scared, or just plain unlucky enough to get crushed. You wouldn't think young people could be so cold, but I guess human cruelty enforces no age requirements.

This morning's duck must have been just a little slow, or maybe distracted by the booming stereo, whatever. And the laughter as they hit the duck and drove away was maybe nervous laughter. A car full of kids, knowing they'd messed up but not knowing what to do to correct the error. So they laughed and drove away.

I think I know most of the cars around our lake and this car didn't belong to anyone I knew. Just kids out cruising and aimlessly reacting to whatever they turn up. I was a teen once. I remember cruising. And you know what? Those boys are somebody's sons. Some mother held them and cradled them and loved them. Some mother loves them still.

Or maybe not. I have to admit I don't know much about teenagers and parents or the particular challenges people face growing up these days. The TV tells me that nearly half of all marriages end in divorce. They say that single parents today are raising one third of kids. They tell me the teenage pregnancy rate is still high and, as a result, children keep on having children. Maybe a dead duck in the road is the very, very, least of our worries these days.

Or maybe not. Maybe these kids came from Ozzie and Harriet homes full of love, and Sunday school. In a way I hope not, because if these kids come from good, stable backgrounds, then where are we?

Do we then have kids crushing the life from a defenseless mallard duck just because they were having a bad week? Riding out a quarrel with some girlfriend? Or angry over some bummer school assignment? And ducks, hey, after all they can fly, can't they? Maybe the duck could have tried harder to get out of the way, you know?

Oh, I am just being silly—silly to want people not to disrespect life. Silly to wish folks would not trash public parks. Silly to want people to not toss beer bottles out windows onto county highways. To not vandalize. To not drink and drive. To not kill in Kosovo.

Maybe it's not so much a matter of boys will be boys as it is a matter of we will be us. Kosovo. Even the word sounds like the crush of bone and feather on concrete.

We live in a violent time. I know it. I don't think that fact of life will soon change. So, today as I carry my shovel back from burying the Mallard duck, all I really ask is one thing.

Cut out the laughter.

It's not so funny. *—April 1999*

# Ritualistic fishermen lured to cove each spring

With the spring the fishermen come back.

In pick-up trucks and four-wheel-drive vehicles they come back reclaiming the lake. They come wearing their final four T-shirts, or not, depending on how the local team did. They come a year fatter, a year slower, a year wiser, or not; depending on how well they adapted to their son's bald-shaved head, their daughter's nose pin piercing, and their wife's new Oprah Book Club.

They come silently. Headlights blinking through April's morning like wild eyes opening from winter's hibernation. One by one they will notice how the great oak fell by the dam. It was February's ice storm that did the killing. One by one they will rub a sore joint, touch a balding head, and mourn the oak. A gray Ford pick up will see the fallen oak and miss his fishing buddy, Jack. Gone to colon cancer. Perhaps it is nothing more than an ice of another kind, but just as fatal to his friend.

Other than a fallen tree and a missing friend's truck, not much else has changed. The lake is still round and green, the rocks still slippery but beautiful when the moon, April's moon, touches and then gives them over to the rising sun. The blue heron still haunts the water's edge, awkward, ragged, and thin from too long a February and March. That one house near the water still smells of bacon and eggs by six a.m. You could set your watch to the aroma. Darn them.

The fishermen both ache and smile tenderly at the breakfast smell. Fishing is smelling. One flannel-shirted fisherman fills his pipe and thinks he smells the hot chocolate he spilled into his tackle box last April. Then he shakes his head. No sir, he'd thrown out that tackle box after Christmas. Maybe it was his smelling that has gone fishing. But just the same, he wished his hot thermos had Nestles Quick instead of Maxwell House this morning.

Someone had set up two new Port-O-Potties near the north and east shores. Silly plastic things painted fake green to look like the great outdoors. Coffins set on edge. Why'd they go and do a darn fool thing like that? Recreation taxes, humpf. You could keep those Johnnies fellas, just stock us some more bass. Or maybe sell hot chocolate from those plastic booths. That would be funny...Port-O-Chocolate.

The two-man boats, left stacked neatly at the water's edge for winter, are launched. Newly charged batteries clamp onto humming trolling motors. Propellers spin like torpedoes fired into spring. Rods and reels clank against the sides of boats waking fish that have slept, eyes open, all the dark winter long. They blink thinking of hooks.

A deer from the woods smells a cigarette and steps back. Her eyes search the mist above the water for the red warning. The glow moves as the fisherman moves, bending to open his tackle box, stretching to cast his first line into spring. The deer understands and will come an hour earlier tomorrow, an hour before the red glow.

Then from the house with bacon and eggs comes music. It is regal, proud. An Italian voice rich and deep fills the lake with opera. Ol Sole Mio. An orchestra balances the tenor's call but cannot match his majesty. The tune is strangely familiar. The fisherman take off their caps trying to place the melody. Italian but so familiar. Is it Elvis? Is this the King back again singing in the spring? It's now or never? *—April 1999*

# Skyline stump bears outline of memories

There is a tree stump at Harmony Cove torn like a city's skyline.

It is an old tree stump—judging by the rings, the living tree stood nearly 100 years. The existing torn-up stump has been resting by the cove for maybe another 50. The interesting thing about this stump, aside from its skyline profile, is the metal marker nailed into the bark. A star-shaped metal piece about the size of a sheriff's badge, it is hammered deep into the wood.

The marker says, "Remember me."

That's all. Not a clue who "me" is or why we should remember him or her. I've been asking around the lake, but nobody knows a thing about "Remember me." One old timer, Bump Hardin, says he first noticed a star like that five decades ago when he and his soon-to-be wife, Faith, were courting.

"Me and Faith used to come down to the lake of an evening for a picnic. Faith liked the peace and quiet of the country around the lake, but she really was a city girl at heart. She and her roommate, Miss Mona Gemm, lived and worked together in Louisville. My Faith was a waitress at the Starglow Diner in downtown Louisville. I visited her there sometimes. It was a noisy, busy place full of factory workers and people who worked downtown. That Faith, she'd bring me fried chicken still hot from the oven.

I'd spread us a blanket and we'd eat 'n smile at one another, you know how young lovers do. Well sir, one evening the sun was setting and Faith stood up to shake out our picnic blanket. I saw a star-shaped thing fall out from the fold of her napkin.

'Honey, what just fell?' I asked. But she just tucked the thing inside her pocket and asked me if I'd like any more dessert."

"So you didn't see the phrase 'remember me' inscribed on the star?" I asked Bump Hardin.

"No sir, not as I remember. But you know, back then I was probably paying more attention to the stars in my Faith's eyes than I was to any old piece of metal. Son, I still miss my Faith. This summer'll be 12 years she's gone. She and Mona Gemm was best friends back then. You might ask Mona about your mystery star. Mona Gemm might recall it."

"You mean old lady Gemm who lives down the south side of the lake?"

"Yes sir. Faith and Mona Gemm were best friends. As I say, they worked together downtown. I never thought I'd get my Faith to ever leave Mona and that city. She and Mona loved city life—the tall buildings, the skyline at night. It came down to me or the skyline and Faith finally picked me.

After our wedding we never saw much of Gemm. Faith quit the diner and then our kids came one right after another. You know how lovers do. But Mona came down for Faith's funeral. She told me at the gravesite she was thinking of moving to Hardin County. Funny thing, too, I never thought Mona would ever leave her city life."

"Why you suppose she came down to Harmony Cove?" I asked Bump Hardin.

"Don't know. Maybe she missed her old friend more than she needed that city skyline. Funny thing, Faith always used to talk about how the skyline looked at sunset. These days when I'm lonely, I drive up to Louisville, cross over the Ohio River and watch the sunset on the tall buildings."

The star is a finely crafted piece of metal. It's hammered just beneath the jagged skyline shaped old stump. If you're interested in seeing it, I guess you have to drive to Louisville with Bump to get a better view. *—July 1999*

## Poolside time capsule preserves time in a bottle

We sit on the screen porch and listen to the hammers and ripsaws. They are tearing down the old wooden deck by the pool. At mid-May, pools all across Hardin County are stirring, being drained, cleaned, scraped, and painted a pale blue. Just around the corner of the calendar is Memorial Day, the traditional "pool-opening day" and unofficial first day of summer.

Our pool down by the west end of the lake is a gem. Patrons, in various stages of tan, can sit gazing out across the smooth green lake as herons and geese coast in the blue sky above. The pool's clear water is a haven for moms, dads, and kids just as the lake is an oasis for the wildlife during summer's heat. It is one of the oldest pools in the area, and that old deck covers a patch of ground that hasn't seen the light of day for many years.

In a way, the deck has been like a time capsule. Slipping through the planks of wood have been the quarters and dimes, Barbie doll accessories, and GI Joe hand grenades of a thousand summers gone by. Can you imagine the number of snow cones and Coppertone drippings that have coated and covered all that time?

Last Saturday night I went for a walk by the pool. I was hoping to find some tokens buried in the exposed ground where the workers had been ripping away at time. I brought my wife's gardening trowel and poked and prodded in the rich damp earth. The ground was a dark loam, almost perfect for planting. Maybe coconut oil and spilled snow-cone suds are a kind of compost mix? Maybe, but I have never seen a bag of potting soil list its active ingredients as: 10% cocoa butter, 15% cow manure, 8% old hotdog buns, and French fries…

I did find some interesting items buried "under the boardwalk." I found a super ball, which still bounced. I found three lenses to sunglasses and one old sunglasses frame. And I found an army of rubber toy soldiers and disregarded dinosaurs. There were checkers (red and black) and Tiddly Winks' chips (blue and yellow) and a whole corral of pastel-colored plastic horses.

I found a teenage boy's red Speedo swimsuit bottoms next to the Playboy centerfold of Miss June of some year back in the seventies. The magazine's page was in decay and all you could recognize was her big round, smile.

There were enough fudgesickle sticks down there to build a life-sized Lincoln log cabin. I guess something about the chocolate preserved them. Or maybe the saliva of an eight year old acts like an Egyptian mummifying ointment. I can't say. But the sticks survived.

I thought my big payday came when I discovered an orange Winnie-the-Pooh hair barrette still clipped to a moldy one-dollar bill. But then, as I was digging around in that thick thatch, knee deep in Popsicle sticks and Barbie doll accessories, my trowel hit something metal. There, up against the pool's concrete outer wall, buried about six inches in the ground, was a round cookie tin.

I was kind of hungry, and past experience with my wife's cooking told me some cookies could survive for decades, so I opened the tin. The inside was cookie-less and smelled oddly like plastic. Not plastic exactly, more like vinyl. The round cookie tin held some papers and an old 45, which back in the Stone Age is what we used to call music records. The disc was in perfect condition, as if it had never been played. It was by the late singer/songwriter Jim Croce.

A yellow newspaper clipping dated September 1973 covered the record. It told of Jim Croce's great success in the early seventies with songs like "Operator" and "Bad, Bad Leroy Brown." The article had pictures of Croce during his days as a college student/ disc jockey at Villanova University. The clipping's headline told about a plane crash that, at age 30, took Croce's life.

I didn't know what to do with my find. I felt as if I'd dug up somebody's bones. But it didn't seem right to just re-bury the record and newspaper. Besides, there was a letter enclosed. On pale blue paper scribbled in a flowery schoolgirl's handwriting it read,

"To the finder. My name is Terri West. Today the evening news said Jim Croce died. He is my favorite singer. It was as if his songs were written to me. My father says the good always die young, and I guess sometimes that's true. I don't know why Jim Croce died. I have a ticket to hear him sing in Louisville next month. Now I don't know what to do with the ticket? My father says the box office will refund my money, but I don't want my money back.

I want Jim Croce back. I guess there's '*never enough time to do the things you want to, once you find them.*' So I am going to bury this ticket and my favorite Croce song under the deck by the pool. It is my wish that whoever you are who finds this that you will listen to the record. Jim Croce was the best. Respectfully yours, Terri West"

Sunday afternoon we are back on the porch overlooking Harmony Cove. The guys down by the pool just finished hammering. And I just finished baking some cookies with real chocolate chips for my wife. The cookies and chips melt in a glass bowl on the table next to two daily newspapers. I tell my wife I read somewhere that chocolate chips have been proven to preserve our youth.

She doesn't believe me very much and says so, biting deeply into a soft, warm cookie. We read. We munch. We are passing the time together. Geese honk out on the lake. Two teen-age girls dressed in hot bikini tops and blue jean bottoms stroll by the water's edge, getting a jump on their summer tans. In a few weeks they will be lounging on the new deck down by the pool.

But today is a peaceful, sun-filled, pre-pool afternoon in mid-May. The two girls stop and look up at our porch and laugh. I guess they could hear my old phonograph re-playing "Time in a Bottle" over and over again. *— May 2000*

# Cuddly cove kittens are yours for the asking

Sometimes people ask, "How can I obtain a piece of Harmony Cove to take home for my family?" Until a few weeks ago I didn't have an answer. Now I have four answers. The shed cats at Harmony Cove have given birth to four wonderful, merry, mischievous kittens.

I have been asked by my neighbors to write this column to find a good home for one, two, three, or all four of the Harmony Cove kittens. These tiny fur-purr balls of love need a good, safe home with loving owners. The four have spunk, and curious personalities and seem very friendly (except for the shy, pale, yellow fellow who hides inside a black coil of plastic drainpipe tubing every time I stop by the tool shed to check.)

You can have these pieces of Harmony Cove (take one, take all?) just by calling the number at the end of this story. But let me tell you about these kittens. Their two mommas (we think two momma cats are sharing a litter) have survived a cold winter in an old tool shed. Neighbors around the cove have kept the momma cats barely alive with scraps of food and pie-tins of cat meal. But it has been a hard winter for the momma cats.

If anyone would like to adopt a momma cat and/or some of the kittens into a loving home, I feel certain they would be fine and loving pets. And unless we can find a home soon for these adorable creatures, I guess the authorities will take them away to the pound.

If you could only see these kittens and two momma cats, you'd see how loving and glorious a part of God's creation they are. In fact what worries me is these two momma cats and their kittens are too trusting, too loving.

They live in a tool shed just off the side of a road winding around the pool and on to Harmony Cove. These cats are so full of love, (and so hungry should our volunteer caregivers miss a day of feed) that they rush out into the road as if to flag down a tender hand to pet them along with a meal for the day.

The two momma cats seem to be able to stop traffic with their big, bright, trusting eyes and more than once I have seen a car or SUV swerve to barely avoid crushing a cat. But the kittens are just getting their leg sense, and, as they follow their momma's out into the road hoping for a meal (and an adoption?) they are less capable in avoiding the big tires.

So I would urge anyone out there who has a big heart and a warm home to call the number at the end of this story and take one of these loving Harmony Cove kittens (and maybe a momma?) to your home.

I'm not saying these cats are anything special just because they live by the cove. But they have survived a hard winter on their own, and so far have managed to avoid the increasing summertime traffic around the lake. They are lucky cats. Maybe if you adopted one, their luck would rub off on you as you petted them?

What I'm worried about is a game I heard four teenaged boys describe called, "crush the kitty." These boys said they didn't like how the cats ran boldly into the street slowing down their cars as they cruised the lake. "Crush the kitty" comes as they speed up scaring the cats to dart away. If the cats escape back to the tool shed, then the cat wins. And if a cat doesn't, well, as one teen boy said, "that'll be car one, cats zero."

This seems like a cruel game. I'm hoping no one really plays such heartless games in our heartland. I suspect this talk was just that, talk, among young bucks—boys wishing to sound studly. And yet, sometimes young people treat small animals unkindly, doing things like shooting birds with BB guns and throwing stones at ducks. (How come it is more often boys and not girls displaying such behavior?) Maybe these young people need to see a model of what civilized and mature adult behavior is like?

But I believe the true test of any civilized society is how that society treats its animals. Do we ignore, torture, and cage our pets? Or, do we embrace all living things with a dignity and respect befitting a creature of God's creation?

I already have two cats, two geese, a stray possum, and I think a stray dog (could be a raccoon—we haven't seen it yet, just heard him) that has adopted me. So there is no more room at my inn. About all I can do is take out a few ads in the paper and write this story.

If you call, I will see to it that someone with a key to the tool shed meets you at your convenience. They'll let you see for yourself how wonderful these kittens and cats are, and you can take home a piece of Harmony Cove that purrs.

I hope someone out there is a cove-cat lover? If you can find a place in your heart and home for one or more of these adorable furry guys, please call me! *—June 2000*

## Pink Fish soccer team is pride of the cove

We have a soccer team at Harmony Cove.

They call themselves the "Pink Fish" and they're cute beyond description. How else but cute could you describe 11 pudgy-legged, five-and six-year-old girls dressed in matching pink T-shirts with a silver fish on the chest. The fish is blowing air bubbles that look like soccer balls.

Cute, I told you.

The girls picked their team name. I helped with the T-shirts. For a while I almost had them sold on the name "Harmony Cove Pirates," and we were going be this fearsome band of blood-spilling, bone-crushing pirates. But the girls wanted pink T-shirts and so the fierce pirate thing sort of faded…

The Skull and Cross Bones just doesn't look good in pink.

I'm the assistant coach of these mighty Pink Fish. This means I carry a bag full of freshly cut orange slices (fish food), and I make sure every girl gets her own water bottle filled with cool (fish-like water don't you know) water for these killer-hot September soccer days.

The boss is Coach Red Herring. Old Red is a former Triple A baseball pitcher for the Pittsburgh Pirates. (See, I had a reason for wanting to call them pirates.) Red is about sixty years old and he has a gut on him like Babe Ruth. He doesn't know a thing about soccer but he has a whistle and a clipboard and the girls love him because he can spit tobacco into a Maxwell House coffee can during games.

I think I could have been coach if I spit better. Lord knows I know more about soccer than Coach Red. But I'm content to carry the orange slices and water bag and occasionally mention to Red the difference between a sweeper and goalie. From time to time I also suggest Red's granddaughter Betty Lynn (he calls her Bubba and she's built just like her grandpa, poor kid) should come out of the game.

"You know Red, give the other Fish…err…a chance to swim?"

"A chance to swim? Hell son, you been sitting in the sun too long…"

Red's not much on assistant coaches or on their metaphors… But I enjoy my duties as assistant coach. Sometimes I have to help the Pink-Fish put on their Fins.

"Fins? Spataro, what in the blue blazes are you talking about, son? I just asked you to help my granddaughter get her shin-guards on. Can you do that? Then maybe you'd better go sit in the shade."

Girls are very particular when it comes to their soccer equipment. We have one girl named Crystal. She asks me to dress her from the knees down every practice and every game. I don't know why her parents can't do this. A teenager in a heavy metal-inspired black T-shirt sits in a dented red Toyota and watches Crystal practice and takes her home. That's about all I've ever seen in the way of Crystal's family. I like Crystal, so I don't mind.

Red waits on practice while I dress Crystal. Red calls her Crinkle. In fact, Red calls all the girls Crinkle except his little Bubba. I don't think Red can see the girl's faces very well, and he refuses to wear those thick glasses he hangs around his neck with fishing line. How in the world he manages to hit that Maxwell House spittoon I don't know...but anyway, he calls all the girls, Crinkle.

Kris Crinkle (that what I call her and she laughs...Ho! Ho! Ho! Like Santa) has a system for getting dressed. First we take off her two sneakers and two socks. Then on goes the left fin (shin-guard), left sock, and left cleat. Then we repeat the process in the exact same order on the right side. I once made the mistake of calling her cleat a mere "shoe" and there was hell to pay.

"No, Coach Chuck, it is not my shoe."

"Huh?" I said holding a moist (how DO little girl's socks get so damp, anyway?) pink sock.

"Cleat. It is called a cleat. Coach Red says we wear cleats, not shoes."

Okay. Cleat. After both fish feet are cleated and ready we count the cleats. It's sort of a song,

"One cleat, two cleats, whose the fish you just can't beat? Who's the fish with cleated feet? Playing soccer's REALLY neat! I'm the greatest Pink Fish you'll ever MEET!"

The best part is when the girls suck their pudgy cheeks in and make a face like a fish.

Another of my assistant coach duties is to "tape" the players before each practice and game. When I coached the Elizabethtown Community College Lady Barons Basketball team I learned to tape ankles while giving my pre-game talk. A community college coach does a lot of things besides coaching, like driving the van to away games and cleaning the E-town Armory after home games. But that's another story.

Taping the Pink-Fish meant putting Band-Aids on any and all boo-boos. The girls have decided Winnie-the-Pooh bandages look best with their pink T-shirts. So I keep plenty of athletic "Pooh" tape in my bag.

Bubba uses a lot of Pooh tape on her knees. The girl is always skinning her knees and bleeding down onto her pretty pink shin-guards.

"Betty Lynn, why do you scrape your knees so much?" I asked.

"'Cause Grandpa makes me play goalie and I keep getting my cleats caught in the net. So I trip."

"Why don't you tell him you trip because your cleats get caught? Maybe he'll move you to sweeper."

"Coach Grandpa says I make his stomach hurt when I tell him stuff."

"Oh."

"Then he has to drink his Presto-Abysmal."

"You mean his Pepto-Bismol?"

"Yeah, that. It makes him get a pink mustache."

"Bubba, grandpa's pink mustache is what we like best about the coach of the mighty Pink-Fish..." *—September 1998*

# The Pisa tree—a leaning legacy

One tree we call the Pisa tree, leans far out into Harmony Cove. Our Pisa tree is a sentry for the changing seasons. It is the first to bud in spring and first to shed leaves in fall. This weekend her leaves began falling as if announcing autumn via so many leaf-shaped postcards floating in the lake's pool.

Leaning alone at the cove's edge, her angle almost exactly mimics Italy's famous stone tower. It is a drawing point to all who share the lake. Bass fishermen sometimes tie their boats to it. Lovers occasionally (not that I'm watching with my high-powered army binoculars) kiss beneath it. And even Old Blue, the ancient Heron who rules our lake, seeks comfort in the Pisa tree's limbs.

It is almost as if the tree calls to us. Part of the call is location. Like a living lighthouse, the Pisa tree commands the high ground at the lake's bank, guarding the very mouth of the cove. And as the sun slips briefly behind a passing cloud it seems as if the tree, and not the sun, lights the cove and sky. "Tourists" first experiencing the Pisa tree's dominance blink and wonder at her power and presence.

As a tourist many falls ago I visited Italy and climbed the famous Leaning Tower of Pisa. It's damp, stone steps are worn with centuries of footsteps: mine, a few hundred thousand tourists, a Pope or two, and the genius Galileo. Each who enters Pisa's tower endures her claustrophobic, narrow stairwell and claws her tomb-cold, stone walls while climbing skyward.

I have been in the Eiffel Tower, the Washington Monument, the Sistine Chapel, and Rupp Arena (sorry, this column is written in Kentucky), but it is Pisa that sticks most in my memory. Something about the twirling dizziness, tight quarters, and unnerving angle of incline has never left me. Each time a cool Kentucky rain dampens my driveway I flash back to Pisa's stone smell, wet and ageless, recalling an atmosphere like human bones.

What impressed me most about the Leaning Tower was its silence. In silence it seemed to say, "I'm still here, and now you have come. I have been here for centuries of Popes, kings, and Galileo. And I'm here for you, now. And I shall be here after all of you are long gone, shivering, covered in the stone dust I shed over you. I stand timelessly waiting for the next season and the next new year."

During my climb I remember hearing a bird's wings fluttering against the stone walls. Was this a poor trapped bird caught inside the walls, or a creature circling the tower seeking sanctuary? The feathers slapping stone echoed in the chamber as I climbed, and today I hear the same rush of wing as Old Blue lifts off into morning's light.

Autumn fills the cove. I see the Blue Heron sailing away and I feel the temperature fall. Today may still be September but the Pisa tree has dropped her leaves. Each sentry knows its own calendar. *— September 2000*

## October is an aging actress

In October the fog rolls across our lake covering the bridge. It hangs like Lincoln Days' cotton candy around my boat tied just off shore. From bridge to boat to shore, fog wraps the cloak of October on all I see. October is this moment. October is this color: black and white in shades of gray vapors so light they float.

My wife tells me this is the most colorful October in years. I say October's color is gray with ghost pale white and stays wet like moss on the wooden bridge. I say before the sun comes up, when the water is not reflected green or gold, is October. I say this chameleon month comes silent in the morning before the sun, before light touches the Maple trees lipping the lake.

I say October is an aging actress, who, using rouge, tricks and colors her face in orange and gold acting witty and gay, but beneath she is mostly pale white. October is a mist, a fog, hiding inside a fishing boat and beneath a bridge's wooden walkway.

I like the colors of October mind you. I like all the oranges and crimsons and yellows. I like gay leaves falling. I enjoy watching the World Series play. I like drinking apple cider and raking leaves to jump in. Oh, the games we play in October.

But I am a morning creature, an early bird that catches the worm. I've seen October before her makeover. I see her sitting on the bridge, her unkempt hair a mess. She's holding a cup of coffee in one hand as the first cigarette of the day draws life between her raw fingers. This is October before the make-up, before the cute pumpkins and Halloween costumes and flannel shirt-ed straw men stuffed with hay.

I see this October in the dawn. With luck by late morning I forget her. By late morning I'm like everyone else: over the rainbow and under the spell of the straw men, with orange pumpkins and costumes of secure super heroes like the Dow Jones and Term Life Insurance and eating my apple a day. It is good the sun comes up chasing we early birds away. Sending the worms and mist to hide deep beneath the bridge, lurking low inside the boats allowing autumn's colored leaves to dance and romp and play.

You and I buy Halloween candy. I stuff straw inside one of my old flannel shirts and borrowing an old Yankee baseball cap I prop up a fat man who smiles like Buddha or Babe Ruth. Both great Bambino's of October. Beneath the Babe I carve pumpkins not for pies but for play. And play counting out October's 31 days. They will come and go, they always do. Ending in a pale, round moon just as the dawn is round and silver fog starts each day.

For now I am the early bird catching the morning rays. The mist wraps round and round the bridge's rails like a holiday wreath in gray. I see the glow of her cigarette on the bridge. I hear her laughter. Fall is crimson after all. *— October 2000*

# "X" marks the spot

Last Friday I was doing some volunteer work at one of our local high schools, when, on a break, I wandered over to the school's library. I grabbed a cinnamon roll, coffee, and a copy of "Collected Poems of Robert Frost." Just as I settled down for a nice snack I overheard someone say, "Oh him? That's Chuck Spataro, he's not from around here. He's from someplace else."

This statement wasn't exactly spoken as praise. It might have been meant as constructive criticism, but, bad as it made me feel, I certainly can't fault it's geographical accuracy. I guess I mistakenly thought once you lived in a place for 23 years, once you'd been married in a local church, nurtured dreams in the local education system for two decades that you became, by proxy or implied edict, "from here."

I'm a dab-blame Kentucky Colonel for goodness sake?

But I guess Hardin County is not home.

"Home," Robert Frost once said, "is the place when you have to go there, they have to take you in." And so, just lately, since overhearing that silly (and probably unimportant) conversation I have been thinking of home.

Exactly where is that anyway?

When I close my eyes and dream of home I remember a pine porch rail, with an intricately constructed "X" enclosed in a box design. I recall looking through that rail when I wasn't yet tall enough to look over it. On that porch I read Treasure Island, dreaming about pirates and treasure maps which always had "X' marking all kinds of important spots.

And somehow that porch rail with the "X" has marked my spot, my home.

It was the rail to a house my Aunt Mary rented at Ship Bottom, New Jersey. We were a block's walk away from the sea, not the "high rent" district to be sure, but close enough as Aunt Mary would say, "to smell the salt off the seabirds' wings."

Some summers, not every summer mind you, but now and then when mom saved up an extra 200 dollars (were things really so cheap in the sixties?), we'd rent the bungalow for a week and sleep with the windows open to the ocean's roar.

At night I'd walk barefoot on sidewalks still warm from the day's sun. We'd fly kites on the beach and fix bicycles tires, the big gawky balloon-sized kind, with patches from kits that smelled like closets full of old sneakers.

Taking a "Ship Bottom shower" meant stripping naked in an outdoor telephone booth-sized stall made of old boards. All the ocean houses had such a shower. Every year sun and salt warped the boards wider apart until it made watching Angela Tozzi's driveway across the street mighty interesting.

Is home the place you first notice the world from? I remember watching many things change (including Angela Tozzi) from behind that porch rail.

But is a porch rail, home?

Maybe not. But I do remember this. Once, after a nasty blow-out caused by jumping my bike onto a piece of jagged driftwood, I didn't have enough money for the tire repair kit. But the drugstore owner (who was Angela's grandmother) told the teenage clerk to "Give the kid the kit, he can pay next time. I know the child; I know his home. He lives in the house with the pirate porch rail."

About that silly cinnamon bun conversation I overheard in the library. The speaker didn't figure on a certain garden rail I have outside my window… —*March 2001*

# A piece of pale malt moonlight

Here at Harmony Cove, some Kentucky moonlight is shining through the baby leaf buds of spring. I can see the moon's malt reflection in the water. Harmony Cove holds the moon like a panhandler's plate, dark and round with a single malt ball in its center. The lake is up and the spillways circling the lake are swollen into tiny lakes of their own. The small wooden bridge I dragged across the lake in my rowboat last year, setting it between the island and the mainland, is covered in spring's thick, green water. It is night and the frogs are singing.

Spring and April are here. These simple things, the swollen spillways, the return of frog-song, and the tiny green leaves budding on our trees surprise me every season. For every year I seem to forget the spring.

I forget the frog song and the Redbud bloom. I forget how the Redbud trees fade and the Dogwoods take their place shaking bubble fragile white blossoms in the wind. All these facts of spring dearly startle me. Maybe it is because winter is so long. Or maybe I have too little faith in the promise of spring.

Can you blame me? We live in a man-made world full of broken oaths. The permanent "I do's" of marriage and the political promises of "I will" often end in divorce and gridlock debate. Whatever the reason, when spring comes, (and it seems to most always come), I watch with the guilt of the unfaithful, or the once faithful but tired. After an April and a May it is easy to expect the summer and a fall. And autumn's golden leaves turning brown and gray announce winter, so memory of winter is not required. But after a long, cold winter, who believes in the promise of new life? Who believes in spring?

On the calendar, January, February, and March appear to last 90 days. But we all know how sometimes February alone lasts six weeks. And March can have a thousand days. When spring comes, and here at Harmony Cove (as it almost always does) it is not something I remember fondly but experience almost unexpectedly, it's always fresh and new like a first spring, a surprise.

Animals are not surprised by spring. They have the faith of instinct that is uncluttered by fearful intelligence. Spring means my cats eagerly ask to sleep outside in the sun and catch baby goldfinches still learning to fly. Spring means the lake birds spin circles in brush piles near shore laying eggs. And unleashed dogs ring the water's edge in search of these sweet yolks for treats. I believe dogs dream of nothing else all winter. Sleeping by the log's fire, they have a fine memory for spring.

I completely forget the spring, forgetting how green it is and how the dandelions toss their seed pods to the wind. I forget how the fish jump in the cove late at evening's light dancing for the sun or snapping at a bug or both or one and then the other one.

All this startles me, although I have seen it come and go, go and come, for nearly half a century. I guess I believe in spring only as the prospector believes in his gold. I hope it will be there in my pan—a nugget, a dream, a piece of pale malt moonlight mixed in water. I swirl all winter searching...sifting... and when it finally comes (so far it always has) I am surprised and almost say the word.

Eureka. *—April 1998*